THE
SOULMATE
LOVER

Also by Mali Apple & Joe Dunn

The Soulmate Experience:
A Practical Guide to Creating Extraordinary Relationships

52 Prescriptions for Happiness:
A Year of Inspiration for the Body, Mind, and Soul

Mantras for Making Love (audio)

Overcoming Jealousy Online Course
(available at www.TheSoulmateExperience.com)

What People Are Saying About
The Soulmate Lover

"The perfect continuation of *The Soulmate Experience,* this is a masterful teaching tool and healing guide that is also a page turner. Reading it together is great foreplay!"
~PATRICK AND SUZANNE CALLAHAN

"With personal narratives, practical applications, and sound relationship advice, *The Soulmate Lover* approaches the topics of sensuality and sexuality in a non-threatening but honest and helpful way. Mali and Joe show people that it is okay to be a sexual being and that sex can be an awakening spiritual experience. Couples often lose touch with each other—this book helps them get their mojo back."
~DR. R. Y. LANGHAM

"*The Soulmate Lover* captivated me right from the start with its elegant flow and simplicity. It is a must-read for anyone seeking a long-lasting and satisfying intimate relationship."
~MIGUEL HERNANDEZ

"Reading this book takes me back to my teenage years when I discovered the sensual-sexual world for the first time. *The Soulmate Lover* is for all of us who believe in the possibility of rediscovering our true sexual potential."
~CLAUDIA KLEIMAN

"This is an 'I can't wait to see what's on the next page' book: informative, eye opening, and could definitely save a marriage or two."
~GEORGE CALDERON

"*The Soulmate Lover* touches on real topics with a thoughtful delicacy. And it doesn't just focus on sex and our bodies. Full of great advice that everyone should hear, it explores ways to enjoy life, build relationships, appreciate ourselves and who we are, and find true happiness."
~MARGARET WARREN

"*The Soulmate Lover* is a lifetime gift for our future. It reminds us to say yes to each other even more and to look at each other with fresh eyes and really see the person we fell in love with. It pulls us up daily whenever we feel the urge to answer for one another and presume something on their behalf. Thank you, Joe and Mali, for these and many other precious gifts."
~KIRSTIE AND DEREK RICHARDSON

THE
SOULMATE
LOVER

A Guide to Passionate and Lasting Love, Sex, and Intimacy

Mali Apple & Joe Dunn

A
HIGHER
POSSIBILIT

San Rafael, California

Published in the United States by A Higher Possibility, San Rafael, California
www.ahigherpossibility.com

Editor: Anna Embree
Author photograph: Dominic Colacchio

Cover image, top: Copyright Voyagerix, 2015. Bottom: Copyright Djgis, 2015. Used
under license from Shutterstock.com.

All the personal stories in this work are true. Identifying details have been changed.

The intent of this book is to offer information of a general nature to readers in the
quest for emotional, physical, and spiritual well-being. The authors are not physicians
or licensed therapists, although members of those professions have been consulted on
certain issues. This book is not a substitute for medical advice or counseling, and the
authors and publisher assume no responsibility for any loss, damage, or malady caused
by the information or lack of information it contains. If you require medical advice or
counseling, please seek the services of a professional.

Publishers Cataloging-in-Publication Data
Apple, Mali.
  The soulmate lover : a guide to passionate and lasting love, sex, and intimacy /
Mali Apple , Joe Dunn.
  p.   cm.
  Includes index.
  ISBN 978-0-9845622-5-1
  1. Love.   2. Sex.   3. Intimacy (Psychology).   4. Interpersonal relations.
I. Dunn, Joseph, 1958–. II. Title.
  BF575 .L8 A68   2015
  158.24—dc23   2014922511

10 9 8 7 6 5 4 3 2 1

First Edition

To Joe

For your unwavering faith, support, and love
For your gentle wisdom and your willingness to play
And for always making me laugh

Mali

To Mali

Thank you for allowing me to be in this place of honor
in your life and helping you get this important
message of love out into the world

Joe

Contents

An Invitation

If you ever feel that there is more to love, sex, and intimacy than you've been experiencing, you're probably right. Whether you're single, dating, or with a partner, if you dream of a relationship that's loving, passionate, and fully alive, this book is your invitation to have just that.

We wrote our first book, *The Soulmate Experience: A Practical Guide to Creating Extraordinary Relationships*, to address the most frequent questions we're asked about how to create a close and connected relationship. We wrote this sequel to go more deeply into questions about how to create and sustain sexual intimacy and desire in order to keep a relationship compelling and passionate. Questions like this:

How can I meet someone who is ready for a
deeply intimate relationship?

If you're looking for a relationship that feels connected on every level, you'll be interested in hearing about the "secrets" taught in a popular (and expensive!) weekend seduction seminar—and more importantly, how to adapt those secrets for the purpose of making a *real* connection with someone. If you're taking your search online, you'll also want to know how to create a dating profile that will attract someone who's really right for you.

The ideas and inspiration in this book will soon have you feeling much more positive about your ability to meet someone with whom you can have a truly intimate relationship.

I've never been able to fully open up sexually.
What suggestions do you have for me?

The truth is, almost every one of us could more fully open to our own sexuality. The explorations in this book will show you how to awaken your senses and your sensuality, feel more positive about your body, connect with your sexual energy, and begin letting go of any sexual shame you might be carrying with you from the past.

As you explore these ideas, you'll naturally begin to feel more comfortable in your body and more confident in your sexuality. You will be more available for deeply connected physical intimacy with your lover. And you might just find yourself experiencing more pleasure than you ever imagined possible.

We have a sexual problem that is affecting our ability
to be intimate. What can we do?

In the chapter on sexual healing, we'll show you how to approach a variety of common sexual issues as opportunities for intimacy and connection. By practicing the art of sexual healing, you'll be able to lovingly address and even dissolve challenges to connecting sexually and, in doing so, create an environment that fosters profound and lasting intimacy.

We've been together for a while now.
How can we keep our sex life passionate and compelling?

Even when we're very much in love, sex with the same partner can become predictable and less frequent over time. The innovative ideas and intimate explorations in this book will energize your sexual connection and bring a spirit of adventure, creativity, and playfulness into the bedroom. This will ensure that even as time goes on, your sex life will continue to be vibrant and satisfying and your passion for each other will stay strong.

Our sex life is already good.
How can we make it exceptional?

The explorations in this book will help you and your lover "supercharge" your sexual connection. For example, you'll learn how to cultivate your sexual energy to heighten your pleasure and deepen your intimacy. As you discover new ways of experiencing pleasure together and open up to your full sexual potential with each other, your entire relationship will feel more connected, compelling, and alive.

I'd love to try some of these ideas, but how can I
get my partner to try them with me?

If you'd like to entice your partner to explore new areas of sexuality with you, or even just try something a little out of the ordinary, you're going to want to know about the power of invitation. You'll find that invitation is one of the most versatile and valuable tools you will ever have. With it, you will be able to ask for many of the things you might desire in your relationship, and in a way that actually inspires more intimacy and love. In our experience, invitation is also the most powerful and effective way to invite your lover to deepen your intimacy on every level: body, mind, heart, and soul.

We believe in the possibility of passionate and lasting love, sex, and intimacy. We believe in this because we're experiencing it, as are countless people we've worked with. This book is our invitation for you—whether you're male or female, gay or straight, single or in a relationship—to experience that possibility for yourself.

In love,

Mali & Joe

1

Sexy Is a State of Mind

At one time or another, most of us have wished we felt more attractive, more desirable, or sexier than we do. But despite what advertisers would have us believe, these aren't qualities you can buy on a dress rack or spray on with a bottle of cologne. They don't depend on your age, your weight, what you wear, or even how you look. More than anything else, feeling attractive, desirable, or sexy is a state of mind.

When Lydia finally accepted Stefanie's invitation to check out the downtown evening market, she was a bit nervous. Stefanie had always said that the market was one of the best places to meet single men, but it had been two years since Lydia had even been out on a date. And it seemed like forever since she'd felt attractive or desirable.

Lydia followed a few steps behind as Stefanie wandered through the array of artists, entertainers, and food vendors. She watched her friend laugh with the man making tacos, recommend lilies to a guy picking out flowers for his fiancé, and even flirt playfully with a couple of police officers selling raffle tickets.

"How do you do it?" Lydia asked Stefanie. "We're the same age, and we look so alike we could be sisters. But you're always so radiant and sexy and I always feel so frumpy."

"Let me tell you a secret," Stefanie said. "To me, sexy isn't about your age or what you look like. It's all about how you're feeling." She took Lydia by the hand. "Here, walk with me. Whatever you thought sexy was, forget it. Pay attention to whatever makes you feel *alive*. It could be the warmth of the sun on your skin, the scent of those lilies, or those crystal earrings shimmering in the sunlight."

They came up to a group of colorfully dressed women dancing to an energetic African beat.

"And when you hear music like this, let it in," Stefanie said. "Forget what anyone else is doing, or what they might be thinking about what you're doing. Just feel the music in your body. Let it *move* you."

Lydia closed her eyes and let herself begin to sway to the sound of the drums. The beat started to take hold, and she could feel herself moving into the rhythm of the dance.

Opening her eyes, Lydia could see that more people were joining in. She felt the evening breeze playing with her hair, bringing goose bumps to her bare skin and a tingle to her entire body. As she turned to catch the last rays of sunlight on her face, she unexpectedly made eye contact with a man standing on the other side of the dancers.

Stefanie leaned toward her. "And when you look in someone's eyes and feel a sense of connection," she whispered, "be open to it."

In the past, Lydia would have gotten nervous and turned away. Instead she held the man's gaze for a few moments. Twenty minutes later, she had a date for coffee—and an entirely new outlook on what it means to feel sexy.

What Lydia discovered that day is a new meaning of the word *sexy*, a meaning that isn't focused on the superficial. Sexy, in this definition, is a feeling of aliveness that comes from within when you are connecting with the sensual world that's all around you.

SEXY: IT'S NOT NECESSARILY WHAT YOU THINK

Say these words to yourself: "I am sexy." If that makes you uncomfortable or even a little embarrassed, let's look at some possible reasons why. Could you have grown up with the idea that people who like feeling sexy are "bad"? Do you recall ever getting the message that you weren't or couldn't be sexy? Are you holding on to an image of what it means to be sexy, like dark and exotic, or young and thin, that you don't match up to? The truth is, there are many more ways to define the word than what we may have learned from our families, friends, society, and the media.

Ian, a photographer, says that what makes his girlfriend sexy to him isn't what she's wearing or even how she looks. "It's her 'life is an adventure' attitude and her willingness to have fun," he says.

"A handsome face, a nice body, and the right clothes can certainly be sexy," smiles Evelyn, a restaurant manager in her thirties. "But more than anything, it's a positive self-image that makes a man sexy."

"I think passion is what makes someone sexy," says Jessie, a graduate student in chemistry. "And that's not only in the bedroom. To me, when a woman is passionate about anything in life, she's sexy."

It Isn't About How You Look—It's About How You Feel

Like Lydia, many of us have bought into the idea that to be attractive, desirable, or sexy, there are certain things we need to do, wear, or say, or a particular attitude we have to adopt. This isn't surprising, given the kinds of messages and images that most of us are inundated with daily.

As Stefanie knows, the key to *being* attractive and desirable is *feeling* attractive and desirable. It doesn't depend on your gender, hair color, age, or shape. It's not about what you're wearing or how much money you make. When it comes to the question of whether you *are* sexy, what's most important is whether you *feel* sexy.

One sure way to start feeling more attractive, desirable, or sexy is to stop evaluating yourself using anybody else's definitions of those words. Instead, start exploring your own ideas of what these words mean. For example, rather than wearing clothes just because they're "in," take time to experiment and discover your own individual style, one that suits your unique face and body and expresses your unique personality.

As you read this book you'll find yourself getting more in touch with who you are and with what feels sexy to *you*. And you'll discover that the sexier and more attractive you feel, the more other people are going to see you that way.

Sexy is not a competition. Sexy is a state of mind.

It Isn't About Your Weight—It's About Being Happy in Your Body

The men and women who have the most satisfying sex lives aren't necessarily those with the most "perfect" bodies, but they are more likely to be comfortable in their bodies. And the more comfortable you are in your body, the more pleasure you'll be able to have with it.

If you are someone who's struggled with their weight, know that weighing more, or less, than you'd like does not prevent you from having an active and very satisfying sex life.

George, whose wife has been overweight all her life, says, "I've always been very attracted to my wife. All of the skin-to-skin contact is quite erotic. We really have a very sexy thing going on."

Julia, a nurse in her mid-forties, says, "I've dated men who are overweight by medical standards. And even though being in better shape would be healthier for them, it honestly doesn't matter to me when it comes down to physical attraction. A man is sexy to me when he likes being in his body."

Marcia has a condition that makes her extremely thin. She and her husband, Dan, laugh about her "negative boobs" and say they make no difference whatsoever in their sexual connection. Dan says that just the fact that Marcia's alive makes her beautiful to him.

Instead of waiting until you're a certain weight or in better shape to feel sexy, why not learn to be a little happier, and feel a little sexier, in your body right now? The ideas and explorations in this book will help you discover how to be more comfortable in your body no matter what its size, shape, or condition. And when you're feeling happy in your body, you'll have a lot more fun being in it.

It Isn't About Your Age—It's About Your Vitality

Almost everywhere we turn, we're bombarded with the message that in order to be sexy, we've got to be young. Yes, youthfulness can be sexy. But as Brandon, who's in his early forties, says, "Anyone with a youthful, positive attitude can be sexy."

The word *vital* means "full of life." Instead of letting age be an indicator of your desirability, why not look to your vitality? This means that rather than focusing on how *old* you are, you focus on how *full of life* you are.

People with real vitality have more energy for living. They tend to be more enthusiastic and more self-assured. Where others see obstacles and problems, they see opportunities and possibilities. They are excited to be alive, open to and accepting of others, and inspired to make the most of whatever time they have. It's not surprising that people with vitality often look and feel younger than they are.

There's not a thing you can do about your age. But there's a lot you can do to increase your vitality.

Ask Your Older, Wiser Self   If you find yourself thinking negatively about your age, imagine yourself many years from now looking back at you today. What does your older, wiser self have to say about the thoughts you're having? One young man reported that his eighty-year-old self advised him, "You don't want to get to be my age and realize how many opportunities you missed. Stop wasting time and get out there!" A woman in her forties received this advice: "There's something to love about *every* stage of life. Find out what it is!"

To start with, take care of your body. We're talking about all the things you already know to do if you want to feel more vibrant and alive. Get enough rest. Eat a healthy diet. Give your body some exercise. Take it easy on the alcohol and drugs. All these factors contribute to how much energy you have and how vital you feel. Consistently taking care of yourself, of course, requires inspiration and willpower—and this book will help you with those.

Vitality, though, isn't just about treating your body well by exercising and eating right. It's also about how you treat yourself in other ways, like making time to pursue what you're passionate about and keeping the negative self-talk to a minimum. The inspiration and ideas we will be sharing will help you in these areas, too.

WHAT MAKES YOU FEEL SEXY?

Take a minute to think about this question: *What makes you feel sexy?* So many things have the potential to feel sexy when we really give them our attention. Consider all of these answers to the question:

- Alisa: "Going salsa dancing with my girlfriends."
- Rick: "Playing a hard game of racquetball and then taking a cold shower."
- Ava: "Driving fast in really hot weather with the windows down."
- Drew: "Wearing my boyfriend's cashmere sweater—and nothing else."
- Lori: "Licking honey off my fingers."

- Tom: "Building a campfire and sleeping under the stars."
- Gabrielle: "Sunning naked on my private patio."
- Jason: "Shaving before going out on Saturday night."
- Susanne: "The intense rush I get from riding on roller coasters."
- Henry: "Lying around in bed on the weekend, reading the paper and drinking good coffee."
- Stephen: "Wearing my best suit for a formal event."
- Claudia: "Splurging on a sexy bra."
- Dara: "Parading around my house in a bikini."
- Sidney: "Feeding my girlfriend sushi."
- Liz: "Wearing a silk dress on a warm summer evening."
- Jackie: "Listening to the blues."
- Keshni: "Seeing my curves in the mirror."

Now how would you answer the question, *What makes you feel sexy?*

Go Through the Magic Door   Here's a powerful technique to help you step out of self-doubt and into self-confidence anytime you want. When you walk through the Magic Door, you choose to accept yourself exactly as you are right now—including your appearance, your personality, and your present life situation. Any door—whether it's the door to your apartment, the door of a restaurant, or even an imaginary door you create on the spot—can serve as a Magic Door. However you happen to look or whatever is going on for you, make the decision to own it. The Magic Door is a way to get in touch with your own magic: the power you have to change your state of mind in an instant. It's your reminder that it's perfectly okay to be you, exactly as you are.

STEPPING INTO A SEXY STATE OF MIND

Life gives you endless opportunities to feel authentically sexy. Here are some ways to make the most of those opportunities:

- *Recognize that you're sexy in your own way.* It's easy to fall into the habit of comparing ourselves to others, but playing the comparison game can be a significant obstacle to feeling good about yourself. Yes, a fit body can be sexy, but so can someone who truly likes being who they are. Sure, stylish or provocative clothing can be sexy, but so can someone who wears clothing they love being in or who carries themselves with confidence and grace. And yes, a youthful face can be sexy, but so can someone who has a joyful or positive attitude. When you catch yourself playing the comparison game, *stop*—and remind yourself that you are unique and sexy in your own way.

- *Show up for a sexy class.* Try some activities that encourage you to explore and enjoy your body in a sensual or playful way. Look for a class that focuses on making a connection between the music and your movement, such as salsa, tango, bachata, ecstatic dance, hip-hop, contact improvisation, or freestyle dance. Or invite a friend to get adventurous with you and take a burlesque, belly dancing, pole dancing, or aerial aerobics class, all of which are designed to help you feel strong and self-confident in your body.

> Stepping into a sexy state of mind makes it easier for you, and everyone else, to experience the sexy in you.

9

- *Have an intention to feel sexy.* Even the most mundane activity can be an opportunity to move into a sexy state of mind. Go for a walk, sit on a rock in the park, or just do the day's errands while devoting that time to experiencing yourself as sexy. Allow yourself to appreciate anything that stimulates your senses or feels the least bit sensual, such as the movement of your body, the smells of nature, or any physical sensations you are experiencing. Just having an intention to feel sexy will provide you with plenty of opportunities to feel sexy more often.

  > Can you feel sexy when no one else is around?
  >
  >

- *Use a sexy mantra.* When you're trying any of these suggestions, you can also incorporate a personal mantra. Try repeating to yourself, "I am sexy and beautiful in my own way," or "I feel sensual and alive," or just "I am sexy." This is simple to do, and it works. When you make a statement like this to yourself, your mind automatically goes to work showing you all the reasons why it's true.

As you put all of these ideas into practice, don't be surprised to find yourself shifting into a very sexy—and very alive—state of mind.

Creating your own definition of what it means to be sexy—or confident, attractive, or any other quality you desire—allows you to own that quality. It also allows others to experience that quality in you. Because when you feel sexy on the inside, it shows on the outside!

2

Sensuality Starts with the Senses

Sharing a sweet strawberry or a lingering kiss, enjoying the simple comfort of holding each other's hand, or just basking in the brilliance of the setting sun—lovers are naturally drawn to connecting through their senses. So opening up and expanding your senses will also open you up to a truly sensual relationship.

"Looking back, I can easily say that Rachel is the most sensual woman I've ever known," Kevin says. "The funny thing is, the first few days we worked together, I hardly noticed her. She didn't dress up the way the other women did; she had more of a casual, down-to-earth way about her."

It wasn't long before Kevin realized there was something quite special about Rachel. "At lunch, instead of heading to the sandwich shop next door like the rest of us, she'd go for a walk. She had this kind of intimacy with plants; she knew what would be in bloom and what was edible, and she'd touch and smell everything. She made that dull business park a fascinating place to hang out."

Twenty years later, Kevin can still remember Rachel's scent. "It was natural and fresh, not something you'd ever find in a bottle. I always tried to get the seat next to her during those long Monday morning meetings."

Kevin wasn't the only person who found Rachel alluring. "Everyone I knew was captivated by her," he says. "That sensual way of hers seemed to just pull you right in."

The truth is, we're all naturally sensual. As children, we're mesmerized by the feeling of soft clay or wet sand. We see sunlight dancing across the floor and run to catch it with our hands. We splash in puddles, bang on pots and pans, bury our fingers in the cat's fur, and squeal out loud with laughter.

Somewhere along the way to adulthood, though, we begin to lose this sensual intimacy with our surroundings. Society, schools, and even our families encourage us to shift our focus from what we're *experiencing with our senses* to what we're *thinking with our minds*. Much of the media, from magazines to movies, pressures us to be more concerned with how we look from the outside than with how we feel on the inside. To make matters worse, the more time we spend with computers, phones, and other electronic devices, the more out of touch with our senses we become. *As we disconnect from our senses, we reduce our ability to connect with others through sensual experiences.*

Try this little exercise: Wherever you are right now, put all your attention on your senses. What do you *hear?* Listen for sounds that are close by as well as sounds that are farther away. What do you *smell?* What do you *see?* Look all around, noticing light, colors, patterns, shapes, shadows. What do you *feel?* Can you sense the chair against your back, the clothing touching your skin, the temperature of the air? Now, what do you notice going on *inside* your body? Can you feel your breath moving in and out? Can you feel your heart beat? Can you feel any sensations of energy, like a slight tingling or pulsing, or a subtle vibration? Close your eyes for a few moments and notice anything else you become aware of.

That's how easy it is to get back in touch with your naturally sensual self: just think a little less, and feel a little more.

MAKE THE MOST OF
YOUR SENSORY EXPERIENCES

Even if you're not a wine lover, you can learn a lot about sensory experiences from people who are.

"Wine tasting is all about using your senses of smell and taste to their fullest," explains Roy, a local wine guru. "And then there's what's called the mouthfeel, the feel of the wine in your mouth. You've got to put your focus on what you're experiencing."

"A good wine is hitting so many pleasure points, it's almost euphoric," Roy says. "Even a mediocre wine can be amazing if you're paying attention."

He likes to tell this story:

"One day a lady came into the tasting room and I poured her the cabernet. She didn't swirl it, she didn't smell it; she just tossed it back like a shot of tequila, made a face, and put the glass back down.

I poured her some more and swirled it around. 'Do you like cherries?' I asked her. 'Yes,' she says. 'Do you like chocolate?' 'Oh, yes.' 'Here, smell this. Do you smell the cherries? Smell the chocolate? Now swish it around in your mouth and kind of chew on it for a few seconds.'

"The lady takes a sip, looks up, and accuses me, 'That's a different wine. You poured me a different wine!' The wine wasn't different. *She* was."

The idea that our *experiences* will be different when *we're* different doesn't apply only to appreciating wine. Whether you and your lover are biting into a mouthwatering mango, shivering under an outdoor shower, or being serenaded by crickets on a hot summer night, let yourselves fully experience whatever you're tasting, smelling, seeing, hearing, or touching. Thoroughly enjoy the burst of aliveness when you first taste that juicy mango, the exhilaration of stepping into that refreshing shower, or the peaceful feeling that comes from listening to those serenading crickets. The more you open up your senses, the more intimate and connected all the time you spend together will be.

Take a Time-Out If you find you're always in a rush, take a twenty-second break now and then to watch the clouds drifting by overhead, inhale the aromas from the nearby cafe, or notice the low murmur of conversation coming from the next office. Giving your full attention to something other than the next item on your to-do list will relax and recharge both your body and mind.

PLAY AT THE EDGES OF YOUR
SENSORY COMFORT ZONES

You may have noticed that when you're newly in love, you're much more willing to experiment and play. A new lover can entice you to try unfamiliar foods, listen to music you've never heard before, or even skinny-dip in a secluded mountain lake.

Gary, a jazz musician, always looks for that kind of willingness in a potential partner. "People can be ruled by their dislikes," he says, "and it makes them rigid and narrow-minded. I've gone out with people who have long lists of 'I don't likes': they won't do this, go here, try that. I find it much more exciting to be with someone who's open-minded, who's more willing to say yes instead of no all the time. Someone who has a real interest in exploring life."

What's Up with All the Nos?

There might be perfectly good reasons why we say no to something. Take food, for example. Some people have allergies or sensitivities. Others avoid certain foods for health, religious, or ethical reasons. And each of us has our own set of taste buds that affects how food tastes to us. Genetics probably even plays a role in some of our food preferences.

But many of our ideas about what we do and don't like are learned. If Andy's family always avoided spicy foods, he's not likely to enjoy them as an adult. If Sophie's parents didn't care for classical music, she might grow up feeling the same way without ever exploring whether that style of music actually appeals to her. We sometimes adopt "I don't like" attitudes in the process of creating an identity for ourselves. For example, someone might announce "I don't care for contemporary art" solely because they think it makes them sound sophisticated.

An "I don't like" belief can also be associated with a negative experience. "My girlfriend insists I'd look good in yellow," says Taylor. "But I've avoided it ever since third grade, when I got teased relentlessly for my yellow sweater."

"The smell of lavender has always reminded me of my grandmother's stuffy sewing room," Christine says, "where I had to sit for hours when I desperately wanted to be outside playing."

Although such associations may be quite strong, *these dislikes are still learned—which means it's possible for us to change them.*

Take a Chance on Yes

Being open to changing your "I don't like" beliefs will make you much more receptive to sensory experiences and the pleasures they can offer. It will also make you more fun to be with. If you can drop the belief that you dislike certain kinds of music, or food, or art, it will be far more enjoyable to stroll the local street festival with your lover, appreciating the variety of ethnic foods and the creative energy of the local artists and musicians.

> **Challenging your "I don't like" beliefs can reward you with some of the most sensual experiences of your life.**

16

You may be wondering whether it's really possible to enjoy something you think you don't. If so, try playing some music from your "I don't like" collection. But this time, really *experience* this piece of music. Pay close attention to everything

Change just one "I don't like" belief and you might be inspired to review your entire list!

you're hearing: voices, instruments, melodies, harmonies. Feel the rhythms running through your body. Focus so completely that your mind doesn't have a chance to remind you, "I hate this song!" You'll discover that there's always something to appreciate about a piece of music you thought you didn't like.

Or take another look at a food you've always avoided because you don't like its taste or texture. It's often just a matter of how fresh the ingredients are or how the food is prepared or seasoned.

"I grew up eating beets from a can," Joel recalls. "I'd quietly slide them into my older brother's napkin, and he'd excuse himself from the table and go flush them down the toilet. Then a few years ago I was served a vegetable I didn't recognize. 'These are *beets?*' I said. 'I never knew beets could taste like this. I *love* beets!'"

The next time you are served a food you "don't like," take this challenge: For a few moments, set aside the idea that you dislike this food and consider the millions of people out there who do enjoy it. As you take your first bite, ask yourself, "How can I taste what they're all tasting?"

Playing at the edges of your sensory comfort zones can sometimes bring unhappy memories and feelings to the surface. Whenever

Christine smelled lavender, the association with her grandmother's sewing room made her feel anxious and claustrophobic. It can be tempting to try to prevent such feelings by simply avoiding the experiences that trigger them. But preventing such emotions from surfacing only keeps them trapped inside us. Until we find a way to process and release them, unresolved emotions will continue to restrict us by making us less flexible and less willing to try something new. So if a sensory experience stirs up uncomfortable feelings in you, see if you can gradually let yourself feel them. Through the process of experiencing them, you will begin to let them go.

When Christine and her husband arrived at a charming country inn and discovered that the linens were scented with lavender, she could have decided it would be impossible for her to stay there. "At first I couldn't stand to be in the room," she says. "Eventually, though, I sat down on the bed and allowed myself to actually feel those old, dusty, claustrophobic feelings. After a while, I noticed there was something more to this scent—a light, summery perfume. And I realized that's probably why my grandmother had lavender in there in the first place: to bring a feeling of the outdoors into that stuffy little attic room."

Open Up to Each Other's Likes   If there's a food your date likes that you don't, take the opportunity to challenge an "I don't like" belief. Taste the food together and see if you can learn to associate this taste with your date's appreciation for it, whether it's the texture, the flavor, or even a pleasant memory it brings up for them. Opening up to each other's likes gives you more of life to enjoy together.

TAKE IT BEYOND
"DINNER AND A MOVIE"

When you make it a point to infuse your dates with sensory experiences, you'll turn what might have been "just another date" into an evening to remember.

Let's start with the dinner part of "dinner and a movie." Sharing a meal is one of the most sensual pleasures on the planet, and creating one together can be its own sensual adventure. Explore the ingredients together. Touch, smell, and taste them. *Look* at them: a tomato or pepper can surprise you with its symmetry. Savor the sensations of rinsing, preparing, and combining the ingredients and the artistry of arranging the food on the plates. When you take the first bite of what you've created together, close your eyes so that the flavors and textures come alive in your mouths.

For dessert, fruits are a deliciously sensual choice. Squeeze some tangy lime juice over slices of velvety papaya or ripe blackberries; drizzle honey or maple syrup onto sweet sections of peach or mango; dip a banana or succulent strawberries into warm, melted chocolate. If there were ever a time to set down your forks and feed each other with your fingers, this would be it.

Instead of a movie, or maybe on the way to one, take your date on a "scentual adventure." Step inside a florist's shop to soak up the intoxicating perfumes. Stroll through the local park, putting your focus on the variety of smells. If you're really paying attention, you'll notice that every flower, every tree, and even every breeze has its own scent.

Because of the way our brains are wired, smells can awaken vivid memories. The scent of coconut, for example, transports Bryan back to the summer he was fifteen. "I was working as a junior lifeguard and had just discovered girls," he confesses. "One whiff of coconut takes me right back to that pool." So if you come across a shop that sells essential oils like lemon, peppermint, cinnamon, or sandalwood, indulge yourselves. The fragrance of a single drop rubbed between your palms can stir up sweet memories and bring a feeling of incredible aliveness and connection to the moment you're sharing.

Opening your senses can turn an everyday encounter into something truly remarkable. The next time you're cuddled up together, whether on a park bench or just in your back yard, close your eyes and *listen*. The sounds around you will instantly intensify, becoming richer and more vibrant. The birds, the voices, the vehicles, and the wind all become instruments in a unique musical composition being played just for the two of you.

And those times you do opt for dinner and a movie, try choosing a restaurant for its sensual food and atmosphere and a film for its breathtaking cinematography or epic music. And let that dinner, and that movie, really move you.

Look to the Stars Few things are as connecting as taking in the magic of a moonrise or a sunset together, so plan a date for a celestial adventure. Get up early to appreciate the beauty of the sunrise. Take a walk by the light of the moon. Or find a spot outdoors where you can curl up in a blanket together and be awed by the vastness of our galaxy.

SENSUAL DATES AREN'T JUST
FOR THE NEWLY DATING

One weekend, Ryan took Heather, his wife of fifteen years, to visit the logging roads where he and his father used to explore.

"Things really hadn't changed much since I was a boy," Ryan says. "As we walked along, more and more memories came flooding back to me. The sound of the river reminded me of the canoe we used to have; the blue wildflowers we always picked for Mom were growing in the same spot. In my mind's eye I could see Dad's much larger hand holding mine, his faded jeans, the old worn-out hiking boots he'd never throw away."

"Visiting this place with Ryan, and experiencing what he used to see and smell and listen to as a boy," Heather says, "connected me to this side of him from the past. I even felt a connection to his dad, who I'd never had a chance to meet. It was a day I'll never forget."

No matter how long you've been together, you can use shared sensual experiences as shortcuts to intimacy. So instead of doing the same old thing on date night, do something that will really engage your senses. Stop in at a teahouse for a tasting. Grab some jackets and get wet in the rain together. Check out local attractions like hiking trails, theater in the park, or music, food, or art festivals. If there's water nearby, go there just to skip some stones

> **Really looking at something together, even a single flower, can be awe-inspiring. And awe is a great ingredient for a date!**

21

and be mesmerized by the ripples and reflections they create. With a little intention, you can turn any date into a sensual date.

And the next time you're out for an evening walk, immerse yourselves in the endless sensuality of life all around you. Open your senses to the moisture in the air, the hum of insects in the distance, the silhouette of the trees against the sky, the rich smell of the earth. Truly appreciate the beauty and the serenity, the feel of the warm hand in yours, and the simple magic of being a couple walking together in the moonlight.

———— ༄ ————

Whether you're with someone new or your lover of twenty years,
connecting through your senses brings sensuality into all that you do,
making every encounter feel richer, more vibrant, and more alive.

3

Accessing Your
Masculine and Feminine Energies

*Whether you're a woman or a man, you have within you the
entire range of human qualities. Think of times when you've
demonstrated qualities like compassion, receptivity, or intuition,
as well as times when you've displayed confidence, willpower,
or courage. Being able to access any of these qualities
whenever you choose allows you to bring more of who you
are to every relationship, especially your intimate ones.*

D ana, a medical researcher, still cringes when she thinks back
to her first few weeks of college.

"This great guy was in a couple of my classes," she recalls. "We'd
laugh a lot and share notes, and I kept hoping he would ask me out.
Then one day another girl just walked up to him and said, 'Hey Jake,
do you want to go to the concert with me Saturday? I have an extra
ticket.' The next thing I knew, they were dating."

Mark, a veterinarian, met Clair at a local singles' night. They dated for several months until one day Clair told Mark it was over. The reason for the breakup, she explained to him, was Mark's habit of declining her invitations to things like visiting art galleries, going on picnics, or seeing the latest romantic movie. Clair loved activities like these, and she'd mentioned to Mark on many occasions that she was reluctant to get into a long-term relationship with someone who had no interest in them.

"I guess I said no one too many times," Mark says. "And it's too bad, because I really liked her. In retrospect, I wish I'd been more willing to try some of her suggestions."

Besides the fact that Dana's and Mark's relationships didn't work out, what do their stories have in common?

If Dana had been more assertive, she might have taken a risk and asked Jake out herself instead of waiting for him to ask her. If Mark had been more receptive to trying the things Clair wanted to share with him, they might both have experienced more of the connection they were looking for.

It's not uncommon for people to be underdeveloped in qualities traditionally associated with the opposite gender. We may also have difficulty accessing the traits typically associated with our own gender.

Jasmine, a sales manager for a growing biotech company, is goal-oriented, confident, and determined. She is a woman who makes things happen. "The problem is," Jasmine says, "I sometimes feel I've lost touch with my femininity. While my husband has always enjoyed my aggressive side in bed, we'd both really love it if once in a while I could just lie back and let *him* take charge. But I can never seem to let go of being in control."

Most people know that having new experiences together, like making love in a different place or in a new position, can help keep a couple's sexual connection feeling fresh and alive. But having new experiences of *each other*, like Jasmine and her husband would have if she could allow herself to relax and be vulnerable, can be far more exciting than just a change of location or position.

As another example, Patrick has been at the same company for almost a decade. He's as talented and productive as any of his coworkers. But while they have all negotiated for raises over the years, Patrick has never summoned the courage to even bring up the subject with his boss. "It just doesn't come easy for me," he says.

Having the ability to access the qualities of confidence and courage would benefit Patrick more than just financially. He might finally get up the nerve to join the local soccer league or to check out the popular singles' events in his city, two things he's wanted to do for a long time.

Identifying and developing those aspects of yourself that you've turned off, or just aren't fully using, gives you access to the entire spectrum of human qualities. It allows you to bring more of yourself to all your relationships, including your intimate ones. Why is bringing more of who you are to your intimate relationships a positive thing? Because you and your partner will be able to connect on many different levels, and your relationship will be more interesting, more rewarding, and ultimately more resilient.

YIN, YANG, AND YOU

The principle of *yin yang* is central to many forms of Chinese martial arts, which encourage the development of both inner (yin) strengths and outer (yang) strengths in order to reach one's highest potential. The yin yang symbol communicates this idea visually: two apparently opposing forces are actually complementary, continually interacting with and supporting each other. When they are operating in harmony, rather than being two separate forces, they become one: a single, unified force.

The symbol also communicates the idea that within yin, there is yang, and within yang, there is yin. For example, compassion is a yin quality, but it often requires summoning one's courage, a yang quality, to act on one's feelings of compassion. Assertiveness is a yang quality, yet it takes intuition and empathy, which are yin qualities, to be able to direct that assertiveness in a way that will result in the best outcome for everyone.

Although many systems of martial arts traditionally encouraged practitioners to develop both yin and yang strengths, the way these disciplines are taught today, especially in Western cultures, emphasizes outer strengths and plays down, or simply ignores, inner strengths. Many sports and other forms of exercise also focus predominantly on outer strengths. Yet watch the most accomplished athletes in any sport and you'll notice that they make full use of both types of qualities. You'll see yang qualities like muscular development, physical strength, and speed as well as yin qualities like flexibility, fluidity, and coordination. There's a beautiful interaction of yin and yang in the movements of any talented dancer, gymnast,

> **By developing both your inner and your outer strengths, you will bring more harmony and balance to your life, your relationships, and the world around you.**

skier, or soccer player—grace versus power, stillness versus motion, softness versus hardness, intuition versus intellect—all operating in continuous, harmonious balance.

What does all this have to do with you?

An inability to access either of these types of qualities, yin or yang, can have detrimental effects on our relationships and our lives. Think of a successful businessman (or businesswoman) who is single-mindedly focused on achieving his goals and has no idea why he can't seem to have an intimate relationship that lasts. Or a brilliant aspiring actor who can easily express any emotion on stage but can't access her (or his) self-confidence or assertiveness to promote herself and her talents.

To function fully in your life and in your relationships, to have integrity and to be a "complete human being," as Chinese philosophers put it, having access to both your inner strengths and your outer strengths is essential.

GENDER CONDITIONING AND
ITS INFLUENCE ON OUR RELATIONSHIPS

More often than not, when we see an infant wrapped in a pink blanket, we will gently coo something like "Oh, look at those beautiful eyes! You're going to be so pretty." If the blanket happens to be blue, we might instead find ourselves saying, "You're such a *big* boy. And your grip is so strong!" Without even knowing for sure whether this little person is male or female, we might find we have a whole collection of assumptions about who he or she is going to be.

Even if we're unaware of it, we often treat young girls and boys quite differently. A girl climbs a tree and we look up and say, "Be careful; that's too high" or "You'd better come down from there. You don't want to fall and get hurt." If it happens to be a boy, we might say, "You're such a monkey—you're so brave to climb that far!" Parents and teachers who make an effort not to treat or talk to children differently based on their gender say they often find the habit challenging to overcome. Despite the movement toward gender equality over the last few decades, many of us still grow up learning that boys shouldn't be sensitive or emotional; they should be strong and brave. Girls are discouraged from being assertive and loud and praised for being gentle and kind.

There are, of course, real differences between males and females. These include physical, genetic, and hormonal differences in both the brain and the body. But our ideas about who boys and girls "should" be go far beyond these actual differences and can influence every aspect of our lives.

Look back at your own childhood. Were you ever discouraged, or even forbidden, from doing something you wanted to do, solely because of your gender? Were you ever discouraged from showing certain emotions because you were a boy or a girl? Can you think of any ways in which those experiences affect who you are today?

Without even being aware of it, many of us learned as children to suppress certain interests or abilities. We may have had passions we didn't pursue because they were considered inappropriate for our gender. Kendra, for example, was discouraged from playing drums and taking woodshop because her parents said they were boys' activities. Zack wasn't allowed to join the tennis team in high school because his dad said tennis was "for sissies." "After three years of wrestling and football," Zack says, "I went to live with my mom so I could try out for tennis my senior year. That year changed me completely. I finally started getting to know who I was instead of who my dad had always told me I should be."

The consequences of gender conditioning on our relationships can be easy to see. Warren grew up hearing time and time again that "big boys don't cry." He feels awkward and uncomfortable when conversations with his girlfriend turn to topics "that might bring up some emotions," he says. In Caitlyn's household, girls were expected to be seen and not heard. As an adult, she often finds it difficult to express her ideas, opinions, and desires. This holds her back from contributing during meetings at work as well as from asking her partner for what she'd *really* like in bed.

Our gender conditioning can also influence how we perceive and

29

relate to others. Imagine a successful litigation attorney who just lost a high-profile case. He decides to console himself with a nice dinner out, as that always helps him to put a loss behind him and get his positive, can-do attitude back. As he enters the restaurant, a woman watching from the other side of the room notices his gloomy look. She quickly sizes him up and whispers to her friend, "Look at him. You can tell just by the way he walks that he's the kind of guy that doesn't know how to get what he wants in life. I'd never be interested in a man like that."

By basing her assessment on the stereotype that men should always appear strong and in control, she completely misjudges his character—and possibly misses out on meeting one of the strongest men she might ever have the chance to know.

OUTER STRENGTHS AND INNER STRENGTHS: WHY YOU WANT TO DEVELOP BOTH

Because of our conditioning, many of us, men and women, grow up thinking of inner strengths as having less value. Yet your inner strengths are every bit as valuable as your outer ones—*especially when it comes to relationships.* In fact, developing both your inner strengths and your outer strengths—what some people call getting in touch with your feminine and masculine energies—will benefit every aspect of your life.

Outer strengths, such as willpower, confidence, discipline, and courage, are useful when you need to take action and deal with unexpected circumstances, like your car breaking down or a storm threatening your home. Having access to these strengths doesn't necessarily mean knowing *how* to fix your car, but rather knowing that, to the best of your abilities, you'll take charge of the situation and find a solution. Outer strengths, such as an ability to see the big picture, can give you invaluable perspective on a situation.

Having access to both your outer and your inner strengths makes it easier to face life's daily challenges and to take advantage of life's daily opportunities.

People who are in touch with this side of themselves will find that it helps them to accomplish anything they set out to do.

Being able to access your outer strengths can also discourage others from trying to take advantage of you.

"When I'm out with my friends, I just seem to be a magnet for all the pushy, annoying guys out there," says Eden, who admits to having difficulty saying no. "I can't figure out why I attract so much more of that kind of attention than my friends do."

When we're unsure of ourselves, as Eden says she often is, we communicate that in many ways, such as through our body language and our facial expressions. Other people, especially those on the lookout for someone who seems easily taken advantage of, will pick up on that insecurity. By accessing the quality of confidence, Eden would be more effective at communicating her personal boundaries—both verbally and nonverbally—and less likely to attract this type of attention.

Inner strengths, such as sensitivity, under-standing, and intuition, are helpful when care and finesse are called for, such as when you're calming an irate customer or comfort-ing a lost child. Being able to access qualities like compassion and empathy are essential in personal relationships; you would use them, for instance, when supporting a friend who's going through a difficult time or offering

Want to summon the courage to ask someone out? Draw on your outer strengths. Want to really connect with them? Draw on your inner strengths.

your teenager the perspective of someone who's been there. Inner strengths are also invaluable in work relationships, whether with your coworkers, your employees, your customers, or your boss. They could be helpful, for example, when you need to bring people together or find solutions that work for everyone.

People who are in touch with their inner strengths have a con-nection to their internal world, including their dreams, passions, emotions, and creativity. They might be sensitive to aesthetics, such as how the placement of furniture and art affect the feeling in a room.

The inner strengths of vulnerability and receptivity are indis-pensable for real intimacy. Vulnerability is the willingness to share yourself authentically with someone else. Receptivity is being open to who another person is in this moment.

As you can see, having access to both your outer and your inner strengths is essential for creating and sustaining a healthy, harmoni-ous, and happy relationship.

ACCESS YOUR OUTER STRENGTHS

If you could benefit by getting more in touch with your outer strengths, begin by looking back to some of the times you've demonstrated these qualities in your life. Can you recall a time when you took charge in a stressful situation? When you summoned more physical strength than you thought you had? Or when you gathered all your courage to do something you were afraid of?

As you reflect on these experiences, feel your own potential for confidence, willpower, and courage. Recognizing that you have these qualities makes it easier to access them when you want to.

Toni, a mother of four, can attest to this. After finding her way out of both an abusive marriage and subsequent homelessness, Toni now appreciates the power of her outer strengths. She says, "What I've learned from these experiences is this: every time I am courageous in the face of a challenge, I grow stronger. Knowing I've survived both of these things makes me realize that I have the willpower and determination to accomplish anything I have dreams of doing."

Here are several more ways to develop your outer strengths, which will increase your ability to access these qualities in any situation:

- *Take on a challenge.* If you don't know how to change your bicycle tire, start a fire, use a certain power tool, or drive a stick shift, have a friend teach you. Try your hand at repairing something instead of assuming you don't have the necessary skills; the Internet has guidance for fixing almost anything.

- *Push yourself physically.* Challenge yourself with an activity that requires a sustained effort, like going on a strenuous hike, digging a hole for a plant or a tree, or taking a spin class. If you're intimidated by the weight-training equipment at your gym, ask a trainer to show you how to use it. Pushing yourself on a regular basis will make it easier to summon your willpower when you really want it.

- *Go it alone.* Try doing things on your own that you'd normally consider doing only with a friend or partner. Going out to dinner by yourself, seeing a movie alone, or making a solo visit to a place you've never been will build self-confidence and self-sufficiency that you can take with you anywhere.

- *Give excess energy an outlet.* Notice when you're about to do something out of a feeling of anxiety, nervousness, or insecurity, and then instead of acting on that feeling, direct your energy into something physical: go on a quick walk or run, spend ten minutes working on a garden or house project, or do anything else that gets your body moving. Physical activity helps dissipate nervous or anxious energy and gives you a little space and time to reflect before you act.

- *Take some downtime.* Give your body opportunities to unwind and recharge, whether that means relaxing with family or friends, doing something just for fun, or hanging out by yourself doing absolutely nothing. Letting everything else go for a while gives your body a chance to refuel.

COME FROM YOUR CENTER

The practice of "coming from your center" can give you access to outer strengths like confidence and willpower anytime you're feeling nervous, uncertain, or insecure.

Martial artists around the world believe that focusing their minds on a spot just below the navel and making their movements from that spot gives their actions intention and power. This area, they believe, is the body's source of *chi*, or life energy. Other people believe that the source of their strength is located in an area of the abdomen known in yoga and other traditions as the third *chakra*, or energy center.

To get a sense of where *your* center is, stand firmly on the ground and rock slowly from side to side and back and forth, feeling for your body's center of gravity and balance. Then close your eyes and feel for the inner source of your power. Don't worry about where martial artists or yogis believe the power center is. Just find the place that feels right to you.

Now practice coming from your center in different situations. Try doing something that requires a burst of energy—like unscrewing a tight lid, lifting a heavy object, or freeing a stuck window—while imagining your effort originating from that area. Experiment with it in situations that make you a little nervous, like speaking up in a group, attending a party alone, or meeting someone for a first date. Move your attention into your center and envision your words and actions originating from there.

Eden, the woman who says she has always had trouble saying no when a man starts pressuring her, has started using this technique when she goes out for the evening with her girlfriends. "When I remember to come from my center," she says, "I find the strength I need to say no in a way he actually hears."

> Coming from your center will help you feel more relaxed and confident in any situation.

ACCESS YOUR INNER STRENGTHS

If you could benefit by getting more in touch with your inner strengths, begin by thinking back to times when you have expressed them in the past. When have you listened to someone else's troubles with sensitivity and understanding? When has your compassion for another person inspired you to do something for them? When has a piece of music, a movie, or a life event moved you to a place of deep sadness or great joy?

Reflect on these experiences for a moment. Can you get a sense of your capacity to be empathetic, compassionate, and sensitive? Recognizing that you have these qualities will make it easier for you to access them—benefiting not only your relationships, but every aspect of your life.

Here are several more ways to develop your inner strengths:

- *Nourish your soul.* Make a list of ten or twenty activities that nourish your soul. When you're feeling out of sorts, pick one of those activities to do, even if only for a few minutes, to help you reconnect with you. If you're thinking that twenty items is too many to think of, here are some activities from other people's lists to get you started: taking a walk in nature; being with animals or children; listening to uplifting music, chanting, or playing an instrument; reading an inspirational book or watching an inspirational movie; meditating or praying; writing or journaling; painting or taking photographs; dancing, running, or doing yoga; volunteering; visiting a new place; spending time with a friend; listening to the sound of the wind or the rain.

- *Get a little sentimental.* Be open to activities that encourage you to feel, like watching a film or listening to music that you find touching or moving. Or allow the memory of a loved one to connect you with your sensitive side by reflecting on how this person still touches your life today: recall stories they told you or things you laughed about, spend time with photos you have of them, or visit a place you used to go together. If these activities (or anything else) happen to bring tears to your eyes, go ahead and cry. Crying is the body's way to relieve tension, release bottled-up emotions, and restore a feeling of balance.

- *Just listen.* This is an especially good practice if you tend to give unsolicited advice or are ever told you're trying to "fix" someone's problems instead of listening to them. The next time someone shares with you a difficulty they're facing, practice just listening. If you find yourself thinking about what you will say in response or what suggestions you could offer, let those thoughts go and refocus on what the person is saying. You might even tell yourself,

"My intention right now is to really listen to this person." You'll be amazed to discover that just listening is often enough to help someone hear their own wisdom and find their own way to an answer.

- *Appreciate beauty—including your own.* Whether or not you notice them, you come across beautiful things all day long: the leaves on the plants you pass by, the child just learning to walk, the light streaming in through a window. Give the beauty that surrounds you a few moments of your attention, and your world will become more beautiful. Also take time to appreciate *your* beauty, both physical beauty and the beauty of who you are as a person. You might even do something in celebration of your own beauty. "For many years I was convinced my nose was too big," says Rebecca. "Now I wear a tiny diamond there to remind me that I am beautiful in my own way—big nose and all."

- *Cultivate friendships.* Get together from time to time with a friend you can really talk to. If you have room for new friends in your life, try out a local activity group: from hiking to photography to writing, these groups are a great way to meet people who have similar interests and, more importantly, are available to explore new friendships.

  If you're a man, you might also consider trying out a men's group. If this conjures up images of secret handshakes and bizarre rituals, relax. We mean the kind of men's group where you get together to share your challenges, learn from each other's experiences, and just generally support each other. "Being in a group with just men, without women to 'posture' in front of," says Darius, "I'm learning to be completely open and to say exactly what's on my mind. It's amazing to reach that level of honest communication about everything."

TAP INTO YOUR INTUITION

Of all the inner strengths, one of the most powerful and yet often underutilized is intuition. Whether you think of intuition as divine guidance or simply as your vastly intelligent mind providing information to you in ways you don't fully understand, it deserves much more trust than it usually gets. Yet you may have been taught to ignore or deny what your intuition is trying to tell you.

The first key to developing your intuition is to learn how your intuition communicates with you. Some people hear intuitive messages in words. Emma distinctly heard the word *Don't!* in her head as she walked down the aisle toward her fiancé. Not long after the wedding, she discovered he was addicted to gambling and physically abusive. The marriage was over within six months.

Intuition can come in other ways, such as through physical sensations. After several dates with Dale, Marcia felt her throat and chest tighten up and her stomach grow uneasy whenever she considered the two of them getting serious. "Even my dreams over those couple of weeks were making me unsettled," she says. "I know from experience not to stay in a relationship when I get these kinds of cues."

Some people get a simple "gut feeling." Tess was driving to her bookkeeping class when, a few miles from school, she had a sudden urge to exit the highway and skip class that evening. Minutes later, a strong earthquake hit the area and collapsed the overpass Tess had been headed toward when she took that last exit. If you're tempted to dismiss this as coincidence, consider that some animals possess an ability to detect upcoming changes in weather, and some may be able to sense impending earthquakes. Is it plausible that humans might be sensitive enough to do so, too? Either way, if Tess hadn't listened to that impulse, she may not have been around to tell the story.

> Intuition often feels like information that's coming from somewhere else.

Here's the second key to developing your intuition: when you have what could be an intuitive impression and there's an opportunity to act on it, *do*. Let go of the urge to question its origin or to evaluate the information; letting your mind jump in with ideas and explanations can interfere with your intuitive guidance. Over time, you'll develop a better sense of whether it's the voice of your intuition speaking or the voice of, for example, your hopes or your fears.

Learning to listen for and act on your intuitive impressions is one of the most valuable skills you can develop for yourself and your relationships.

Terence found himself dating one man after another who had serious addiction issues. For years he insisted that he was always surprised and that there were never any warning signs.

"I finally realized that wasn't true," he says. "I *was* picking up on signals that a particular person might not be good for me. I just didn't want to hear them, so I'd ignore them and tell myself I was just feeling nervous. Now I'm listening—I've had enough drama and heartache for a lifetime."

Turning down the noise in your life—like switching off computers, phones, and televisions when you can, or quieting an overly active mind through meditation or other practices—can make hearing your intuition much easier. You can also try accessing your intuitive guidance directly. Ask yourself a question like *What is there for me to know about this?* or *What's the best thing for me to do in this situation?* Then listen for an answer, in whatever form it might come to you: in words, a feeling or impression, a physical sensation, or even later in a dream.

Ask Your Body Every cell in your body is highly intelligent, and the different parts of your body are in constant communication through a network of nerves and chemical messengers. Is it possible, then, that your body might know something about what's wrong with you even when you don't? It may recognize, for example, that your stomach has gotten upset every time you've eaten a certain food, even if your mind hasn't yet made that connection.

Try asking your body what's going on: *Why are you in pain? Where's this pain coming from? Why are you feeling so exhausted?* See if you get any impressions about what's happening or what you might do to help. For example, you might get an impulse to massage that part of your body, to drink more water, or to ease up on a certain activity for a while. Give your body a chance to communicate with you, and you might be surprised by what you learn.

As you develop your intuition, you'll find yourself relying on it more and more. You'll also discover that it's indispensable for navigating life's constantly changing conditions. After all, when was the last time you heard someone complain, "If only I *hadn't* listened to my intuition!"

THE BALANCE OF YIN AND YANG IN RELATIONSHIPS

The balance of yin and yang isn't important just within an individual; it's also important in a group. In a successful sports team, for example, each player is keenly aware of what the others are doing and skillfully contributes his or her own abilities to the team effort. In an accomplished musical group, the musicians interact as a harmonious whole: listening to each other, supporting each other, blending their individual interpretations of the music to create something beautiful.

The same is true for a group of two. A couple's relationship can be richer, fuller, and more harmonious if they are each aware and supportive of what they and their partner have to contribute.

Victor and Jolene were together for more than ten years when they decided to start a small online business. They are both quite talented, but whenever they tried to collaborate on designing their new website, things quickly turned uncomfortable. Jolene, the more business-minded of the two, is very aware of the need to accomplish tasks in a timely manner to meet their business objectives.

Victor, who is more of an artist, is most creative when working on his own. Their very different styles made it difficult for them to work together. Anxious to accomplish whatever it was they had set out to do, Jolene would get impatient. As soon as Victor felt her impatience starting up, he says, "I would start to shut down."

The couple made very little progress on their new business—until Jolene finally realized that expecting Victor to operate at her pace was counterproductive.

"I've learned that the more I relax and allow him to create at his own pace, the more we actually get done," she says. "And the more fun we have in the process."

In Jolene and Victor's story, we can also see the yin yang concept of each type of strength or energy supporting the other. From Victor, Jolene is learning how to open up to her yin side and bring some balance to her own predominantly yang approach: "When I get to a point where I'm struggling, I actually hear his voice in my head saying, 'Relax. Just let it come.' And by relaxing, I find that my creative energy gets replenished and I'm once again in the flow." Victor has found that the yang characteristic of setting goals helps him to direct his creative yin energy and accomplish more than he ever thought possible.

> Relationships are a whole lot easier once we realize that we're all from the same planet.

Jolene and Victor have discovered for themselves that one of the greatest gifts two people can give each other is encouragement to open to all their strengths, both inner and outer. Their story also reflects the great wisdom illustrated in the ancient symbol: when the yin and the yang, the feminine and the masculine energies, are in harmonious, dynamic balance, they become a unified force that is capable of achieving great things.

———————— ✿ ————————

The more you and your partner can each access the full spectrum of human qualities, the more of yourselves you will be able to bring to every experience. This ability allows you each to realize your full potential as a human being and gives your relationship unlimited opportunities for connection and growth.

4

Letting Go of Sexual Shame

*If you've ever felt guilty, anxious, or troubled around any aspect
of your sexuality—such as your body, your desires, an incident
from the past, or a situation you're in currently—it could be
that you're carrying around some degree of sexual shame. This
can make it difficult to open up and express yourself with a lover
and prevent you from experiencing your full sexual potential.
Learning how to identify and release sexual shame makes you
available for a deeply connected relationship.*

"I am finally starting to open up to my full sexuality."

Jenna, a property manager for a vacation rental company, has
had three significant relationships in her adult life. When she turned
thirty, Jenna says, "I found myself reflecting back on them. My boy-
friends were all great guys. But no matter how much I loved them,
I just could never feel comfortable sexually. I finally realized that
my own discomfort around sex was the main reason why all three
relationships ended."

Jenna decided to share her realization with a couple of her closest friends "so that I didn't have to keep it all to myself," she says. With her friends' support, she soon got to the core of why she could never just let go and enjoy being intimate with a man she loved.

"By sharing them with my friends, I was able to go into those places where I felt embarrassed and confused, where I was hiding aspects of my sexuality," Jenna says. "I was able to unravel the layers one by one to see what was holding me back. What I came to understand is that I was ashamed for being too sexy or too sexual, so I was covering it up and pretending I wasn't that. I was raised believing that I shouldn't look sexy, that I shouldn't be sexual. It just wasn't okay to enjoy or even be curious about sex."

In facing her feelings of shame and embarrassment, Jenna says, "I had to struggle with the question of whether being a sexual person was inherently good or bad. I know what people back home would think. People get scared and become defensive and judgmental when they can tell you enjoy being a sexual person, so I learned to repress that part of me."

Instead of hiding her natural sexuality, Jenna says, "what I really needed to do was to accept it, embrace it, and explore it. Now I'm starting to allow myself plenty of opportunities to experience my sexuality, to explore my desires, and to appreciate my own unique beauty."

Today, instead of hiding behind dark, conservative ("and uncomfortable!") clothing in an effort not to call attention to herself, Jenna wears fabrics and colors that express her sensuality and her appreciation of her own body. She also takes classes in massage "to intentionally spend time immersed in touching."

Jenna is very much looking forward to her next relationship. "I no longer feel a need to pretend I'm not a sexual person," she says. "I am finally ready to bring my full self to every experience. No more hiding!"

As Jenna discovered, feelings of shame can have serious effects on our intimate relationships. Shame can cause us to feel inhibited, embarrassed, or unworthy. It might express itself as avoidance, anxiety, anger, or withdrawal. Until we investigate, we may have no idea just how much shame can influence us.

We can feel shame around just about anything: how we dress, speak, or act; our family or our upbringing; our education, occupation, or income. For example, despite the fact that he owns a successful appliance business, William feels ashamed that he never graduated from high school. Caroline is embarrassed about her tendency to binge eat whenever she's feeling overwhelmed. Isabelle has felt out of place at formal parties and other events ever since she was a teenager. "Like I might embarrass myself at any moment," she says.

Shame is often used intentionally to try to affect other people's behavior. Parents use shame to keep their kids in line. Advertisers use shame to get people to buy their products. Adults use shame to influence or manipulate other adults, including friends, relatives, coworkers, and yes, even partners.

Although any type of shame can affect our sexuality, shame around our bodies, our desires and fantasies, or our sexual history and experience (or lack of experience) affects us the most. Anita has always felt inadequate for being "skinny and flat chested"; Stuart feels "embarrassed about my small size, if you know what I mean." Lawrence is uncomfortable being naked in front of his girlfriend "because nudity was just not okay when I was growing up," while Serena's fear of intimacy is strongly linked to "the shame I feel about being overweight." Dave is reluctant to share with his wife of fifteen years "my fantasies of her tying me up and having her way with me." Mitchell, who's now in his sixties, feels ashamed about the way he used to treat women when he was in his twenties and thirties. And Doug, a twenty-nine-year-old virgin, feels so much shame around his inexperience that at this point, he says, "I can't even imagine ever actually having sex."

SEXUAL SHAME: IT'S HARD TO REACH ADULTHOOD WITHOUT IT

Rarely are we taught how to have connected, satisfying sexual relationships. Most of us grow up hearing a jumble of mixed messages about sex, especially about what's acceptable and what's not. Our families, schools, churches, and society in general often avoid honest discussions of sexual issues. Negative experiences as adolescents, such as being teased or bullied for being gay (whether or not we actually are) or being labeled a "slut" or a "whore," can sow the seeds of sexual shame. Parents who are uncomfortable with their own sexuality often unknowingly pass their inhibitions on to their children. Intentionally or not, they send the message that sexual thoughts, desires, and actions are bad, wrong, or even evil. Pornography can also cause people to develop feelings of shame (we talk more about this in Chapter 8).

As a result of all these experiences, we learn to suppress, hide, or even reject our sexual nature, such as our desires or interests. We may find it difficult to set healthy boundaries for ourselves. It's no surprise that we are often unable to bring our whole selves to a sexual relationship.

Gavin, an aspiring actor in his thirties, confesses, "I feel guilty every time I have sex. I even feel guilty when I'm just feeling *attracted* to a woman."

Gavin can see that the way his family treated him when he was growing up contributed significantly to his discomfort around women and sex. "The first time I was ever attracted to a girl, at fifteen, my family teased me mercilessly," Gavin recalls. "From then on, my mom and dad made fun of me whenever they thought I liked a girl, so I learned to hide any interest I had in anyone. Once I started dating, I could only bring myself to ask out women I *wasn't* really attracted to—and I'd end up feeling guilty about *that*."

Shame can also be the result of awkward, unwanted, or abusive sexual experiences. Abuse in particular can cause deep-seated, long-lasting shame that can affect us our entire lives unless we take steps to address it, whether that's with the help of a counselor or therapist, in a group setting, or in our own way.

Healing from sexual shame gives you more freedom to enjoy your sexuality and your intimate relationships.

49

LETTING GO OF SEXUAL SHAME

Even a little bit of shame can negatively affect both your life and your relationships, so uncovering and addressing any shame you might be carrying will make true intimacy much more possible for you. Healing from sexual shame usually involves some combination of the following steps:

Step 1: Recognize and Investigate Your Shame

We often don't realize we're being affected by shame until we start to look for it. Just being aware that you are experiencing even a small amount of shame is the first step toward letting it go.

Once you recognize that you're having feelings of shame, you can do a little investigation. For example, maybe a particular issue or a certain situation has come up, and you realize you're suddenly feeling awkward, inhibited, or embarrassed. You might ask yourself these questions: *When and where did I first experience these feelings? In what kinds of circumstances do they arise? What have they prevented me from doing?*

If you find that your shame is associated with something you can't change (like an incident that occurred when you were young, a physical characteristic you have, or something that happened against your will), recognize that you're not at fault; you've done nothing wrong. If you're experiencing guilt because of something you did, learn what you can from it, make amends if possible, and then begin to let the guilt go by understanding that continuing to carry this burden is not helpful to you or anyone else.

Step 2: Challenge the Thoughts and Beliefs Underlying Your Shame

Next, look for any negative thoughts or beliefs underlying your shame and try "upgrading" them.

For example, Serena, who has a fear of intimacy because of her weight, might be telling herself something like "I should be thinner." Whenever she notices herself thinking that, she could try replacing that thought with "No matter what weight I happen to be, I am still lovable."

Lawrence, who is uncomfortable being naked in front of his girl-friend, might have a belief like "Nudity is not okay" operating. He could try reminding himself that "Nudity is natural—we're all born that way" or "It's okay for me to be naked, especially when I'm with the woman I love."

Doug, who feels shame because of his inexperience, might be thinking something like "Nobody's ever going to want to have sex with me," which would only make him feel even *more* nervous and awkward around women. He could try telling himself instead, "I know there's *someone* out there who will see beyond my nervousness and want to get to know me."

> Your thoughts and beliefs don't always have your best interests at heart.

Reprogramming your negative thoughts with more positive ones is a powerful practice that can improve your experience in every area of your life. Yes, this takes awareness and intention, but the rewards are well worth it.

51

Step 3: Shine Some Light on Your Shame

It's virtually impossible to heal something that you keep hidden away. So once you've uncovered any feelings, memories, thoughts, or beliefs associated with your shame, consider sharing them with a trusted friend, a counselor or therapist, or a support group. This takes courage, but just being heard and understood by another human being can be immensely healing. If you've been through sexually traumatic experiences, you may want to go one step further and see someone who specializes in this area.

Sharing your shame with a loving and receptive partner will not only help free you from it; the process of sharing will also bring the two of you closer together.

Dave, who was embarrassed about his fantasies of his wife dominating him sexually, was encouraged by a counselor to find a way to tell her about them. At first, he says, she was taken by surprise: Dave is a very strong man who manages a large company and trains regularly at the gym. Eventually, though, she came to understand why he might want to relinquish control once in a while, and she agreed to try out some of his ideas.

"Just being able to *talk* to Amy about this made me feel so close to her," Dave says. "The fact that she was willing to try—well, that's just icing on the cake."

Trevor, who is in his late thirties, was sexually abused as a child. Those early experiences caused him, as an adult, to back away whenever he started to feel close to a woman. In the past few years, he has begun the process of healing from his childhood experiences. He has shared his story with several friends and feels that, for him, it is also important to do so with anyone he's considering being intimate with.

> Anything you bring out of the dark and shine some light on will have much less power over you.

"With a potential partner, I like to have a conversation about my sexual history and my patterns in my previous relationships," Trevor says. "This makes it so much easier to notice if I start to pull away from her and to communicate about it if I do. It sets the tone for us to be really open as sexual partners. I honestly don't *want* to be sexually intimate with someone I'm not able to have this kind of conversation with."

Step 4: Reduce Your Sensitivity to Your Shame Triggers

When you understand how your shame gets triggered, you may be able to gradually desensitize yourself to the circumstances that bring it on. Look for ways to ease yourself into situations that trigger your discomfort so that you can slowly acclimate to them.

For example, Lawrence, who is uncomfortable with his girlfriend seeing him naked, could start by spending time with her in the nude, first in the dark and then gradually turning up the lights as he gets more comfortable. Or how about making a sexy game out of it by laughing together through a few hands of strip poker?

Gavin, who feels shame even when he's just attracted to a woman, works part time as a waiter. "My job gives me an excuse to practice going up and actually talking to women I find attractive," he says. "I've even recently found the courage to ask one of them out."

53

IT'S NEVER TOO LATE TO
LET GO OF SHAME

Jennifer, a personal trainer, began to heal from the source of her sexual shame at the age of fifty-two. We can see many of the steps of letting go of shame in her healing process.

"Sex for me has never been about intimacy and connectedness and love," she says. "It's always been something I used to get what I wanted. I've been nothing more than a performer. In fact, I just ended a two-year relationship where I faked every orgasm."

Determined to change her pattern with men and uncover what was preventing her from experiencing real intimacy, Jennifer began seeing a counselor who specializes in relationship issues. Soon she found herself talking about the sexual abuse she and her sister had suffered at the hands of their older brother—events she hadn't spoken to anyone about for decades. With the counselor's help, she began to see how her abusive childhood experiences had affected every romantic relationship she'd ever had.

"To try to get my brother's love, I did what he wanted even though it felt bad," she says. "And that became my pattern with men. My body was a lure. I learned to use my sexual talents to try and get things like acceptance and appreciation. But I always ended up feeling used."

Bringing our shame out into the open, as Jennifer did by sharing with her counselor the memories and feelings surrounding her past abuse, may lead us to want to talk with other people in our lives about our experiences. Though her brother had died several years earlier, Jennifer eventually had conversations with both her sister and her mother about being sexually abused as a child.

"The more I talked about it, the more it let go of me," she says. "Sharing my experiences, and how they affected me throughout my life, really helped to neutralize the shame that I've had attached to those memories. I just can't fake it anymore. I've made a commitment to be true to myself."

Jennifer has also made an important discovery about the adverse effects of keeping shameful feelings and memories locked up inside.

"Although the abuse I experienced as a child lasted only a few months," she says, "hiding it has negatively affected every relationship I've had since."

Jennifer believes that bringing her secrets out into the open is what has made healing from her past possible.

"I'm finally ready for a real, grown-up sexual relationship," she says. "I'm excited. It's as if I'm a fifty-two-year-old virgin!"

As we let go of shame, we no longer have to hide parts of ourselves.
Though we may never rid ourselves of all our feelings of shame,
as we grow in acceptance of ourselves as sexual beings—including
our bodies, our desires, and our pasts—space will open up for
true and lasting intimacy.

5

Inspiration for Getting Off Your A** and Into Your Body

The better care you take of your body, the more confident and comfortable you'll feel with a lover. Yet if you're like most of us, at times you struggle to treat your body in ways that will keep it strong and healthy. Often the answer to this struggle isn't a new diet or exercise plan, but finding new ways to stay inspired and motivated. So if you could use inspiration for taking care of your body, this chapter is for you.

"I think we should stop seeing each other."

These eight words sent Anika into a depression that lasted two long years. As the months dragged on, she stopped seeing friends and took up smoking again. She quit the aerobics class she used to love and frequently found herself bingeing on chocolate and ice cream. In less than a year, she'd gained thirty pounds.

Anika would go to work, then come home to sit in front of the television. The talk shows and reality dramas helped to drown out the discouraging voice in her head that tormented her with thoughts like "I'll never have that kind of love again" or "If I'd been sexier, smarter, better in bed, we'd still be together."

Then one day, a friend insisted on taking her to a yoga class. It took almost more willpower than Anika had just to get up and put exercise clothes on.

The class began with a simple meditation. Closing her eyes, Anika could hear the all-too-familiar voice growing louder. The feelings of worthlessness and despair that always accompanied it welled up inside of her.

After a few minutes, the instructor asked everyone to stand. With a soothing tone, she said, "Now I'd like you each to find yourself in the mirror." Anika looked up, terrified by what she was going to see. "As you look deeply into your eyes, acknowledge and accept that this, right now, is who you are. And that this, right here, is the perfect place for you to be."

The instant Anika gazed into her own tired eyes, they filled with tears. In that moment, she says, "I realized I didn't accept anything at all about the worn-down woman looking back at me. Afraid I was going to fall apart, I was just about to pick up my stuff and leave when we started the first pose."

The next hour was so physically challenging that Anika couldn't stay stuck in her head, churning through her gloomy thoughts about the love she'd lost and what an undesirable woman she was. Anika walked out of the class exhausted—and feeling better than she had in a long time.

That one hour was the turning point for Anika. She began to show up for the class three times a week. It wasn't long before she noticed that all the sweets were making her feel sluggish and tired. Anika also found that now she had enough willpower to start making better choices for herself. After a few weeks, she gave up the cigarettes and began seeing friends again.

Today, Anika has some valuable insight into how she finally broke through her depression.

"Getting into my body was the ticket out of my head and out of my depression," she says. "Now I know that when I'm not doing yoga or some other activity regularly, I'm not as motivated, I can't think as clearly, and my body starts to drag. Once I start spiraling downward, it's more and more of an effort to get to class. I've learned that it's easier to go consistently when I remind myself that this *one step*, this *one hour* of physical activity, will get me back in my body and make all the difference."

OUR BODIES ARE MEANT TO MOVE

Watch children for a few minutes and you'll see that they use their entire bodies when they play. They go after a ball with everything they've got. The moment they hear music, their bodies start to wiggle and shake. They're always finding new ways to move: hopping, twirling, rolling, and waving their arms around just because it feels good.

What stops us from moving with such freedom and ease as we get older?

To start with, there's self-consciousness. From as young as two or three, we begin to have thoughts about what other people might be thinking about us—from how we look to what we do and say to our beliefs and ideas. Many of us even develop an invisible audience: an idea that someone is always watching us and judging our actions and behavior, even when we're alone. As we become more self-conscious, we're less and less comfortable moving and playing freely.

In addition, as we age we tend to get into routines and narrow our range of physical activity. Over time, we lose strength and flexibility and become less comfortable in our bodies. And this is if we're active at all. With the demands of adulthood, the prevalence of desk jobs, and the ability to shop, socialize, and be entertained all without leaving our chairs, it's easy to become quite sedentary. The longer we spend just sitting, the further we get from that natural ease of movement we had as children.

Our bodies are designed to move. For one thing, movement activates endorphins, those magical little hormones that reduce anxiety and stress, lower blood pressure, strengthen the immune system, and slow the aging process.

Want a better sex life? Start by doing some kind of exercise. Regular exercise will reward you with strength, flexibility, and endurance and have you feeling more confident, more self-accepting, and just better overall. It also increases testosterone (in men *and* women), raising your energy levels and your sex drive.

If you ever find yourself struggling with a low sex drive, you might try exercising your way back to desire!

There's no getting around the fact that great sex requires physical effort. If you don't want to wear yourself out in the first three minutes—not to mention going for round two!—do whatever you can to be in the best shape possible.

> The more playful you are in your body, the more playful you'll be in bed.

MAINTAINING YOUR MOTIVATION: HOW TO OVERCOME INERTIA AND GET OFF THE COUCH

If even the best athletes can have trouble staying motivated, how are the rest of us supposed to remain inspired to keep our bodies moving?

Ask any athlete, and you'll discover that he or she has a collection of tools to keep them motivated—and they will go find new ones when the old ones stop working. So here is a wealth of great ways to motivate yourself when you're finding it hard to get your body in motion and need some new inspiration:

- *Talk to yourself like a friend.* If you find it hard to motivate yourself to even get out of your chair, much less to a demanding yoga class, retrain your mind to give you *encouraging* messages instead of *discouraging* ones. When you realize you're thinking, "I'll never be able to keep up" or "I'll look so out of place," instead say to yourself, "Everyone has to start somewhere" or "Whatever I do is better than doing nothing at all!" This is especially helpful in group exercise classes, where it's very easy to start comparing yourself with others and quickly feel inadequate and discouraged. And tell your body every once in a while, "Thank you for everything you've allowed me to do. I'm going to take the best care of you that I can." A little appreciation and intention today make it much more likely you'll say yes to physical activity tomorrow.

- *Quiet those discouraging thoughts.* Sometimes it's just simple worries, like whether you will be able to keep up or how you are going to look, that stop you from exercising. If this is ever an issue for you, start to pay attention to how those thoughts make you feel; just becoming aware of their effects will help quiet or even eliminate them. In addition, any activity that's sufficiently challenging can help you break through a negative thought pattern. Anika found the yoga class so physically demanding that she had no choice but to take her attention off her negative thoughts and put it on what her body was doing.

> The more you appreciate all your body does for you, the better you will feel *in* it.

- *Use the buddy system.* Find a friend to work out with, even if it's only once a week. (And don't let anyone convince you that doing

---

Make It Your Reminder   Here's a way to make your self-critical voice work for you rather than against you: turn self-criticism into a reminder of something positive you've been wanting to do for yourself. If you sit for hours at a computer, for example, you could make that negative voice your cue to stand up and stretch, rest your eyes, or get a glass of water. Your negative thoughts will fade into the background for a while, and your body and mind will be grateful.

---

something only once a week is ineffective. Doing something fifty-two times a year is infinitely better than doing it no times a year.) Exercising with a friend is about more than just having someone to encourage you; you're their support system as well. "Having a workout buddy is motivating," says Sarah, a busy college student. "I show up because I don't want to let *him* down." Show up regularly for a kickboxing or Latin dance class, a triathlon training group, or a boot camp workout program, and you'll soon have a whole community of people supporting you in your endeavors. And if you can find ways to exercise with your lover, the shared effort can deepen your physical connection.

- *Make it a meditation.* Take your workout one moment at a time. To get moving, tell yourself, "All I'm doing right now is tying my shoes. All I'm doing right now is filling my water bottle. All I'm doing right now is walking out the door." As you begin to move, pay attention to what's happening inside. Feel your muscles warming up, your lungs expanding as you breathe, the breeze cooling your skin. Then, if your mind starts to give you messages like "This is hard! I don't like this. I want to stop *now!*" narrow your focus down to what you're doing moment by moment. Put all of your attention on what you're feeling, like your feet hitting the ground, or your muscles stretching, or the rhythm of your breathing. By making your workout a meditation, you'll be able to do far more with less effort. If your mind tries to convince you to quit early, tell yourself you're going to walk, run, swim, or whatever it is for just one minute more. "I sometimes say,

'Come on, Ari, just another thirty seconds' ten or twenty times over the course of a run," Ariana says, "and before I know it I've gone two miles."

- *Be your own cheerleader.* For Ranisha, the secret to keeping herself motivated is to encourage herself as she goes. "I'm always telling myself, 'You can do it. You're gonna make it. It's not that much farther. You've done it before!'" Giving yourself positive messages will make those ideas start to take root in your subconscious, eventually making exercise easier. Also develop a habit of checking in with yourself regularly: "Is that actual pain I'm feeling or just my muscles tiring?" If it's just exertion you're feeling, breathe into the sensations, reminding yourself, "That's not pain, that's discomfort." Or "This is what it feels like to get stronger." Your brain will eventually get the message that this feeling isn't "bad uncomfortable," it's "good uncomfortable." Finally, your approach to exercise can mean the difference between following through or not. "Throughout the day, I try to focus on how much I will enjoy going to yoga," says Warren. "That way a strong desire to get to class is programmed into my mind." Anna says, "I like to make an exercise plan for the next day. Otherwise, when tomorrow gets here, I'll just do what's easiest—which may mean nothing at all."

> Having compassion for your body and all it goes through can be powerful motivation for taking better care of it.

- *Choose media that motivates you.* It's hard to avoid the video screens that fill so many gyms these days, but they might not be the best thing for your workout. Although their purpose is to keep you entertained, they may have the unintended effect of disconnecting you from what you're doing. And putting your primary focus on something other than your body can result in ineffective, lackluster workouts. So if you want to incorporate media into your exercise routine, choose something that complements what you're doing. Experiment with different kinds of music or audiobooks to find something that's really motivating and also allows you to stay tuned in to your body.

- *Use an exercise mantra.* When your mind is resisting the idea of exercise, it will come up with an endless stream of excuses for you. That's where a mantra can help. If you're arguing with yourself about whether or not to work out, or you find that you're making excuses like "I'm tired" or "I'm not seeing any changes," try motivating yourself with an inspirational phrase. Josh's personal workout mantra is "I *always* feel better after I exercise." Sophie reminds herself that "the better care I take of my body, the more I enjoy sex." Heidi actually programs her phone to flash at her, "Want a tight butt? Get it to the gym!" Or try one of these: "I don't *have* to work out, I *get* to work out." "I'm just one workout away from feeling great." "Exercise today—feel stronger and sexier tomorrow."

  > Taking care of your body can be its own spiritual practice.
  >
  > ☙

- *Mix it up.* If your typical excuse for not exercising is "It's boring," add some variety. New activities not only reduce boredom; they strengthen muscles you don't normally use and improve balance, flexibility, and coordination.

There are so many physical activities out there to try, and more are being invented every day. Do a little research and take a class in something you've been curious about or have never even heard of. Have you ever considered hooping, slacklining, or aerial fitness? If you're single, know that activities like these are some of the best ways to meet people who still want to play.

A willingness to play is a very attractive quality!

- *Do something every day.* Whether it's your weekly dance class, a walk with the dog, or just stretching while watching the news, commit to doing one thing each day. "I make myself do something every day," says Shannon, "but I get to choose what that something is. Giving myself that flexibility, and only doing things I really enjoy, makes it much easier to fit some type of exercise into my day." Lila, who is in her seventies, sometimes exercises twice a day. "You might have arthritis, you might have an injury or two; it doesn't matter," she insists. "You just gotta do whatever you can do!"

If getting to a gym or studio is a challenge, check out some of the thousands of free instructional videos online. You'll find plenty of inspiring, well-produced videos for virtually every kind of exercise there is. They'll have you belly dancing in no time.

- *Water yourself regularly.* Every cell in your body depends on a steady supply of water to function properly. Staying hydrated also keeps your skin and hair looking younger and healthier. To help yourself remember to drink enough, make it a habit to have water with your meals and to carry a water bottle everywhere you go. When you're at a stoplight, take a quick drink instead of checking your phone. And taking two large mouthfuls instead of just a sip is a simple habit to get into that makes staying hydrated much easier.

- *Feed yourself well.* It's no secret that the better you feed yourself, the better you'll feel. For many of us, though, the number one criteria for what to put into our mouths is *Does it taste good?* But in a world of processed foods, taste is not always a reliable indicator of whether a food is actually good for you. Processed foods have been manipulated to appeal to our taste buds while their nutritional quality has plummeted. They may contain added salt, sweeteners, artificial colors and flavors, preservatives, genetically modified organisms (GMOs), residues from pesticides and herbicides, and chemicals leached from containers. These additives may well be contributing to such health issues as asthma, allergies, obesity, diabetes, heart disease, and cancer.

Because we think it tastes good, we often try to ignore how an unhealthy meal makes us feel. But if you want your body to be operating at its peak, or even close to that, you have to put as much attention on how foods feel as on how they taste.

Have patience with your taste buds. The body craves what it has been trained to crave.

As you become more aware of the negative effects a food or drink has on you, you'll find it easier to choose a piece of fruit over a croissant, a handful of nuts over a cookie, or a glass of juice (or something more exotic, like kombucha) over that second glass of wine.

GIVE YOUR BODY
PERMISSION TO PLAY

When was the last time you allowed your body to hop, skip, shake, or wiggle? Try wiggling right now. How natural does it feel to you? To be more confident and comfortable in your body, you may just need to forget about what others might say and give yourself permission to *play*.

Here are several easy ways to "channel your inner child" that will soon have you feeling like a kid again:

- *Play with your sense of balance.* Besides helping to prevent injury, a good sense of balance improves coordination and posture, making it an excellent antidote for the effects of aging. It also increases self-confidence, which is great to have at any age.

Try this: Stand up and place one foot directly in front of the other, as though you're standing on a line. Now close your eyes. Can you keep your balance for ten seconds? You might be surprised at how challenging this is.

Feeling confident and comfortable in your body might be the most potent aphrodisiac around.

68

Balance is something you can play with anywhere. While you're waiting in line, brushing your teeth, or getting dressed, see if you can balance on one leg or just lightly rest one foot on top of the other. If you start to wobble, picture the whole planet under your foot supporting you, and you will immediately feel more stable. As you get better at balancing on one foot, try shifting your weight around, circling your lifted leg in the air, or closing your eyes. And the next time you see those funny balance toys at the gym, ask someone to show you how to play with them.

- *Stretch whatever you can, wherever you are.* Just like playing with balance, stretching is something you can do almost anywhere: neck rolls on the ride to work, calf stretches while waiting for the elevator, wrist and shoulder circles at your desk. If you're worried what people will think, just know that your example might be the perfect reminder for someone else to stretch. Or listen to Kathy, a regular stretcher: "When I see someone stretching, I think, cool, there's someone who cares about their body." Have a few playthings around the house—straps or bands, a balancing ball, a foam roller— and actually use them. Instead of just sitting down for television, get on the floor and work out some of the kinks from your day while you watch. Get the full benefit from any stretch by taking several slow, deep breaths into those areas that feel the tightest. When you get the hang of it, a deep stretch can feel amazing.

  Flexibility: great for your body, awesome for your sex life.

69

- *Free your inner dancer.* Dancing without planned steps or move-ments encourages your body to move in new ways and frees you from having to worry about whether you're "doing it right." Put on some music you particularly like. Start to move, but instead of directing your movements with your mind, allow the music to move you. Let the familiar rhythms and melodies expand out into every part of your body. This free-form movement doesn't have to look like anything in particular; it could resemble stretching, or aerobics, or even martial arts. If you find yourself distracted by thoughts about how you look, try picking out just one instrument, voice, or sound to follow to give your mind something useful to do. Get your body moving in new ways by experimenting with a variety of music, from classical and jazz to reggae and hip-hop.

- *Immerse yourself in water—the perfect place to let your body play.* Water offers just the right amount of resistance and support for every movement. If you have access to a heated pool or a hot tub, take advantage of it (if you can go without a suit, even better). When you're immersed in this warm, supportive environment, enjoy the deliciously sensual feeling of the water flowing over you as you explore moving in every way you can. And if the hot tub has a jet, let your body enjoy the benefits of that too.

All of these ideas for letting your body play are also wonderful ways to connect with a lover. Have fun trying to keep your bal-ance while walking along a curb, stretching out each other's tight muscles, dancing together in the bedroom, or floating each other around in some warm, sensuous water.

"Staying physically connected is very important for maintaining our sexual connection," says Miguel about his relationship. "It's a way for us to stay playful, feel sexy, and have fun as a couple."

IF YOU'RE NOT USING IT, RELAX IT

If you often feel tired during the day, know that feeling more rested doesn't necessarily require getting more sleep. Right now, check in with your body. Are there any muscles in your face, your neck, your shoulders, or your back that could be a little more relaxed? Intentionally let those areas go. You might be surprised by the number of places where you're holding tension.

Most of us could be a lot more relaxed than we are. Throughout the day, we tend to contract many more muscles than we actually need for everyday tasks like sitting, standing, and walking. There's no reason for the muscles in your face to be tight or your shoulders to be scrunched up to your ears while you're working at your desk.

We could take a lesson from top athletes, who expend energy only as needed. They continually scan their bodies to ensure they're engaging only the muscles required in that moment. A champion swimmer, for example, might periodically ask herself, "Is my neck relaxed? Are my shoulders loose? Am I being as efficient as possible? Is everything moving in harmony—my arms, my legs, my breathing?"

This is a great practice to use anytime: Whether you're sitting, walking, or working out, simply scan your body from head to toe, checking to see if each body part is as relaxed as it can be for what it's doing. When you find a place that's tense or tight, take a deep breath into that area, expanding it with your inhale and letting it soften with your exhale.

Whatever you're doing, can you do it with 5 percent less effort?

You might also give your whole body opportunities to completely relax, even if for only a few moments at a time. Sit fully supported, or lie down on a bed or the floor, and just let go. Take five or ten breaths, relaxing a little more with each one. A minute or two of complete relaxation, spread throughout your day, can be surprisingly energizing.

And whatever you're doing, see if you can do it in an easy, fluid, and relaxed way. Get in the habit of asking yourself this question: *Am I doing this activity with as little effort as possible?* Just think: If you saved 5 or 10 percent of your energy throughout your day, you'd have that much more to put toward other things you really love—including your love life.

———— ❀ ————

The more you get into your body—by taking the best care of it you can while appreciating the body you have right now— the more comfortable and playful you'll be in it. And the more comfortable and playful you feel, the more connection, pleasure, and just plain fun you're going to have with a lover.

6

Connecting with Your Sexual Energy

Whether you're single, dating, or in a relationship, exploring your
sexuality will keep you sexually vibrant. If you're single, getting
in touch with your sexual energy will make it easier to recognize
someone with whom you can have a truly satisfying intimate
relationship. If you're with a partner, it will help you continually
create an experience of profound passion and intimacy.

"Sex just wasn't important to him." Miranda, a physical therapist, ended a three-year relationship after trying everything she could think of to entice her boyfriend into the bedroom more often. He finally admitted to her that he'd just never had much of a sex drive.

"He also was very clear that he had no interest in looking into *why* his libido was so low," she says. "I eventually had to say good-bye, because I'm at a point in my life where exploring sexuality is very important to me."

Miranda is excited about the prospect of being with a man who *is* enthusiastic about exploring sexually with her, and she has no doubt she soon will be. For the moment, though, she's quite happy to be single and on her own.

"I'm really enjoying being with myself," she says. "I'm treating myself to little luxuries, like taking long, steamy hot baths. Or going out to dinner on my own, just relaxing and having conversations with anyone who seems interesting."

Miranda says she feels more in touch with her body than she has in a long time.

"I recently took up yoga, and I'm loving the feeling of growing stronger and more flexible," she says. "It's really given me confidence."

She's also had fun shopping for sexy new lingerie. "And I'm not waiting for a new man in my life before I enjoy them. I'm doing things like turning up the music and dancing around my kitchen while I make dinner—in nothing but my bra and panties!"

Since she's not seeing anyone at the moment, Miranda has also been taking the time to explore her body and what brings it pleasure. In fact, she says she feels more sexually satisfied than she has in years.

"I'm having so much fun right now that sometimes I think, why do I even *need* a man?" she laughs. "Seriously, though, when he finally shows up, I'm going to be ready!"

Trenton, who married his high school sweetheart and still enjoys "a very strong sexual connection" with her, also speaks candidly about the importance of staying in touch with his sexuality.

"A loving, passionate sexual relationship is one of the most incredible experiences in life," he says. "So it's important to me to do whatever I can to maintain that passion."

For one thing, he works out daily "to keep my body in the best shape I can for her." He goes shirtless around the house and in the yard whenever possible: "It makes me much more aware of my body and how I'm sitting or standing or moving." When he gets a chance, he also spends time being nude in the sun. "I enjoy the warmth," he says, "and the feeling of being completely at ease with myself."

Unlike Miranda, though, who enjoys pleasuring herself, Trenton doesn't masturbate very often.

"When I was younger, I would pretty much do it any chance I could," he laughs. "These days I'd rather save my sexual energy for getting creative in the bedroom with my wife. And I find that when my sexual energy is high, I have much less interest in masturbating anyway."

Although these two stories are quite different on the surface, they do have something in common. Miranda and Trenton both know that staying in touch with your sexuality—whether you're single or in a relationship—keeps you feeling vibrant and alive.

SO JUST WHAT IS SEXUALITY, ANYWAY?

You've probably noticed that some people seem to have a sexual aura about them. Take a moment to think of someone you know who seems very connected to their sexuality. Can you see it in the way they move? In the way they interact with others or their environment? How is it reflected in their body, their personality, or their outlook on life?

Edie is a woman who seems to just exude sexuality. She turns heads and makes new friends wherever she goes. It's not that she's trying to get attention; she simply stands out because she's comfortable in her own skin and truly enjoys getting to know new people.

When you think about men or women—or even couples—who have a strong sexual presence, it might prompt you to ask, *Just what is sexuality?*

People often define sexuality quite narrowly: "Sexuality is intercourse and everything that leads up to it." "Sexuality is anything related to your sexual organs. That pretty much covers it."

These kinds of limited definitions make Edie smile knowingly.

"My own definition of sexuality really has very little to do with the sex act," she explains. "It's more about how I feel about myself, my self-confidence in being who I am—whether I'm alone or with someone else. It's also about just enjoying being in my body."

You'll notice some similarities among people who are in touch with their sexuality. In general, they like being in their bodies, which makes them less self-conscious and more self-assured. Whether it's sharing a meal with friends, going for a walk in nature, or making love, they take time to enjoy life's simple pleasures. Because they know that the world is full of beauty and mystery, they bring a sense of curiosity and adventure to their entire lives, especially their sexuality.

Robert, who is in his forties, is a man many women identify as having a strong sexual presence. It's interesting to hear his perspective on sexuality.

"Sexuality isn't something we can put into a box and say, well, that's sex," he says. "From a purely biological perspective, of course, we're wired to want to connect with another human being in a deeply physical way. Intercourse is the most extreme example of this, but every small movement toward that—whether it's looking into someone's eyes, a gentle touch, or breathing someone else's breath—contains that desire to connect and can be considered an aspect of sexuality."

Like Edie, Robert thinks of sexuality in an expansive way. "Sex, to me, is being willing to be changed by an interaction with someone. You go in vulnerable and open, and when you connect in that way, you come out changed—whether that's sexually, emotionally, or maybe in your perspective about something. Being that open can be scary; we're always trying to protect ourselves. But it makes sexuality very alive."

By expanding your idea of what sexuality is, you take sex out of the box. And when you do that, you will naturally be more adventurous and creative, and your sexual experiences will be richer, more meaningful, and much more pleasurable.

Everything you've explored in this book so far—giving yourself permission to feel sexy more often, activating your senses and your sensuality, opening up to your masculine and feminine energies, being in touch with your body, and letting go of sexual shame—is an aspect of connecting with your sexual energy. Whether you're male or female, single or in a relationship, the explorations that follow will inspire you to continue that process of opening up.

You can think of sexual energy as life energy channeled into your sexuality.

77

EXPAND YOUR PERCEPTION
OF BEAUTY

The next time you're sitting in a public place like a cafe, see if you can notice something attractive or beautiful in every person—male or female—who passes by. Whether it's their eyes, their smile, or the way they hold themselves, find something to appreciate in each person you see. This simple exercise, and those that follow, will allow you to see more beauty not only in other people, but also in yourself.

Immerse Yourself in a Single Image

Begin this exploration by selecting a picture of a man or a woman, like an artfully done nude or a sensual image from a fashion magazine. A simple black and white photograph is an especially good choice. Now relax and give yourself plenty of time to take in all the details: skin tone, muscles, textures, colors, shades, symmetry, shadows, the light falling on various areas. Follow along any contours and curves with your eyes. Also notice the spaces *around* the subject. Take in the photograph as a whole, as a single piece of art. Really try to *feel* the image rather than *think* about it. If you notice yourself making judgments or comparisons, see if you can simply let them go.

> By deepening your appreciation of the human body, you'll become more aware of the beauty in others as well as in yourself.

As you explore this single image, you will probably find yourself discovering more and more about it that strikes you as sensual, beautiful, or alluring. Try this exercise again from time to time and with photographs of both women and men. You'll find that the deeper you look, the more beauty you will see.

This is also a wonderfully intimate exploration to do with a lover, sharing each new curve, shadow, or subtle detail you discover in a particular photograph. You'll both have a greater appreciation for what you're seeing—not only in the photograph itself, but in each other. If you and your lover are feeling close and connected, this can also be very intimate to do with photos of yourselves. You'll be surprised to discover how much beauty there is in a photo you thought was "no good."

Connect with Your Reflection

When we look in a mirror, many of us see ourselves in pretty much the same way every time or focus only on what we don't like. In this exploration, which is best to save for a time when you're feeling adventurous, you will learn to see yourself in new ways.

Have both a hand mirror and a larger or full-length mirror available. Starting with the lights low, or using just candlelight, begin to explore your reflection just as you did with the photograph in the earlier exercise.

If this is difficult to do without negative judgments coming up, look at your reflection as though it's someone you don't know but are curious about. Or try looking in the hand mirror at your image reflected in the larger mirror.

Healthy self-appreciation can do wonders for your sex life.

Turn Your Body into Art   Having some sensual images of yourself can help you to see yourself as beautiful. Have a close friend or a professional photographer take "boudoir" pictures of you wearing something that you feel attractive and desirable in. (Nude photographs can also be a wonderful way to celebrate your body. But do be careful: any image you share electronically can never be taken back or permanently deleted.) Remember to take your images out from time to time as a reminder to yourself of all the beauty in your own body.

This can help you see yourself with less judgment, as the perspective will be different from the reflection you see every day.

Slowly move around, viewing your reflection from new angles and letting your gaze fall on one detail at a time. This could be the curve of your hip as you twist your torso, the way the light accentuates the muscles in your legs or shoulders, or the line of your jaw seen from a certain angle. Notice curves, muscles, and smooth areas of your skin. Try to find something to appreciate in everything you see, even things you'd typically be quick to overlook or reject.

GET GOOD AT BEING NAKED

This might sound obvious, but the more comfortable you are being naked, the more comfortable you'll be when you're with a lover.

Some people are perfectly relaxed in the buff almost anywhere, while others feel awkward or shy even when they're by themselves. There are many reasons why someone might be uncomfortable naked. They might have grown up in a home or a culture where nudity was unacceptable or associated only with sexuality. They might have been teased, ridiculed, or otherwise gotten the message that their body, or a particular part of it, was not a desirable shape or size. Or they might simply have very little experience with being naked.

Ariel, who describes herself as skinny, was told early on by her father that "real women have curves." She has never been comfortable naked, even around her female friends.

Negative sexual experiences, especially abusive ones, can also leave us feeling insecure. A man Lynn dated in medical school once made a comment about her "muffin-top breasts," and she's been worried about their appearance ever since.

Being truly comfortable naked requires a certain degree of self-acceptance—which you can develop through practice. Trenton, for example, who says that spending time without a shirt on helps him stay connected to his body and his sexuality, also says the practice has made him more self-accepting.

You don't have to have a "perfect" body to feel perfectly comfortable in your body.

If being naked is an issue for you, the next time you're standing in a warm shower, close your eyes and concentrate on the feeling of the water as it sprays against your skin and streams down the contours of your body. Move around, noticing how that changes the sensations you're experiencing. If you have any worries or anxieties about your body, you might even imagine the water washing them away.

In addition to addressing any feelings of shame you might have around being naked (see Chapter 4), try these dos and don'ts for feeling confident and relaxed when all you're wearing is your birthday suit:

- *Don't focus on your "flaws."* Often what's in the way of feeling comfortable naked is nothing more than the thoughts you're having about what you've decided is not okay about your body. When you notice you're thinking such thoughts, break the cycle by turning your attention to something you appreciate about your body and thinking about that instead. For example, a woman who's thinking "I hate my legs" might spend a few moments remembering all that her legs have allowed her to do in her life.

- *Do focus on the feeling.* You can find people of every shape and size who are perfectly happy being naked. Part of their secret is that they tend to focus less on how they *look* and more on how they *feel*. There's a great sense of freedom in being unrestricted by clothing, in having nothing between you and your environment. Being naked is just plain sensuous. The more you focus on that feeling of sensuousness, instead of on how you look, the more you're going to enjoy being naked.

- *Don't compare yourself.* It may seem ironic that we have more and more nudity in our society and less and less comfort *being* nude. But many of the images we see of other people's bodies have been digitally altered, and it's easy to compare ourselves to those unrealistic "ideals" and feel lacking or self-conscious. If this sounds familiar, consider cutting back on movies, shows, or magazines that make you feel inadequate. And by conducting a little research into just how much manipulation is done to photographs of models and celebrities, you will come to understand that the faces and bodies you're comparing yourself to are *just not real.*

- *Do be nice.* Make this pledge: *When I'm naked, I'll do my very best not to criticize myself.* Anna says, "I frequently look in the mirror when I'm naked and think, you know, that's not so bad. I'd rather be slimmer, but I can be okay with this." You probably won't let go of all your negative self-talk, but it's possible to drop a substantial amount by becoming aware of just how pointless and even harmful it is.

The more time you spend in the nude, the more natural being naked will feel. So following are some ways to put those dos and don'ts into practice. Just be sensible, which includes checking for any legal restrictions on nudity where you live.

It's easy to find ways to get more "naked time" in the comfort of your own home. If you usually wear pajamas to bed, trade them in for silky sheets or a warm comforter that feels soft and smooth against your bare skin. Try walking around your bedroom without clothes, focusing on the feeling of having nothing between your skin and the air or between your feet and the floor. Open a window to feel the breeze on areas of your body that are usually covered. Is the air a little chilly? See if you can interpret the sensations as stimulating or exciting.

> **Any time you spend worrying about how you *look* naked is time you can't enjoy *being* naked.**

If you're alone, venture out into the living room or kitchen. Does being naked in a place you're usually dressed make you nervous? Now try interpreting *that* feeling as stimulating or exciting. Naomi says, "Doing dishes in the nude is a sexy way to get some housecleaning done." How about putting on some music and dancing naked? Or, if you have access to a private, secluded area outdoors, step outside and experience the sun and the wind—or the rain!—on your skin.

If you're in a safe environment, being naked in the presence of other people can be a healing experience. (By "safe environment," we don't mean a college drinking party or a bar!) Do you belong to an exercise studio or a gym? The locker room can be a good place to practice getting more comfortable with your bare body, especially if you use the opportunity to let go of any self-criticism that comes up. If possible, visit a spa and treat your body to an unusual experience— like a mud bath, a hot stone massage, or a body wrap—with the goal of thoroughly enjoying all the sensations that arise. Seek out a Japanese-style bathhouse, where men and women usually bathe separately. The traditional ritual involves washing your entire body before relaxing in the sauna, taking an invigorating dip in the cold plunge, sweating in the steam room, and just drifting in the warm-water pool. Or spend some time with a good friend at a clothing-optional beach or hot spring. Even if you choose to wear a bathing suit initially, you'll grow more comfortable once you see the variety of bodies and realize there's a lot less judging going on than you might have imagined.

If you're already pretty good at being naked, expand your comfort zone and volunteer to be a model for a life-drawing class, where *all* bodies are works of art. You'll come away knowing that being naked in a roomful of people who are studying every inch of your unclothed body is really no big deal.

INCREASE YOUR SENSITIVITY TO TOUCH

Millions of nerve endings and other receptors allow your skin to sense pressure, texture, vibration, pain, and temperature. The explorations that follow will deepen your appreciation for your incredible sense of touch, making both *touching* and *being touched* all the more pleasurable.

Begin by tracing your fingers up and down your arm. As you do, concentrate on all the different sensations you're experiencing from the perspective of the skin on your arm. You might even imagine that it's someone else's fingers that are touching you.

After a minute or so, shift your focus to the perspective of your fingers. Concentrate on what your fingers are feeling rather than on what your skin is feeling. You might even imagine that it's someone else's body you are touching.

Now see if you're able to follow the sensations in both your arm and your fingers at the same time. This takes focus and is very helpful for developing your sensitivity to touch.

Experiment with different kinds of touch. Rub some oil or lotion over your entire body, enjoying the sensuous feeling. Explore erogenous zones like your ears, your neck, your inner thighs, or your toes. Caress your skin with a silk scarf; tickle yourself with a fingernail, a feather, or the tip of a toothpick; paint your body with an ice cube.

Can you touch yourself in ways that build a little anticipation? Can you give yourself goose bumps or cause yourself to shiver? Can you find ways to make that state of anticipation last a little while?

Can you give yourself goose bumps just by *thinking* about them?

Sensation is one aspect of sexual energy, one part of your "sexual system." The more attention you pay to any sensations you're feeling, the more heightened, stimulating, and enjoyable they'll become.

SEXUAL ENERGY AND THE ART OF SELF-PLEASURE

When used in a healthy way, masturbation is considered by many experts to be a positive aspect of sexuality for singles as well as those in a relationship. For one thing, self-pleasuring can help us to become more comfortable with our sexuality. It can contribute to sexual well-being in single people who are waiting until they are in a committed relationship to enjoy their full sexuality. And it can help anyone stay connected to their ever-changing body and desires.

Some people, of course, have religious, spiritual, or other reasons for abstaining from masturbation. If this is you, you may still find some ideas here worth considering. And if you feel any shame around the thought of masturbation, you might look back at Chapter 4, "Letting Go of Sexual Shame."

You'll notice that none of these ideas involve sitting in front of a computer screen. Just as pornography can become a substitute for being intimate with a partner, it can also let you avoid being intimate with yourself (the topic of pornography is explored in more depth near the end of Chapter 8). So if you're accustomed to watching or reading erotic material while self-pleasuring, turn off the computer, put away the books and magazines, and get comfortable.

Sexual Self-Intimacy

Give some thought to these questions: *What would masturbation be like if you'd never done it before? If you knew it was perfectly natural and healthy? If you were turned on by your own body? If you could completely let go?* When you bring a spirit of acceptance, adventure, and playfulness to masturbation, you will naturally bring those same qualities into your sexual relationship with another person.

Self-pleasure can be about much more than stimulating yourself to reach orgasm. It can, for instance, be as simple as just enjoying your body's state of arousal. This is something you can tune in to whenever you're immersed in a sensory environment. Soak in a warm bath, float in an inner tube, or luxuriate in the feeling of the sun touching your skin, taking in the experience through all your senses. Enjoy

> Can you find a way to enjoy self-pleasuring more than you ever have before?

the motion of the water, the movement of the air, the beads of sweat forming on your skin, the delicious feeling of your body letting go.

The more creative you are with self-pleasure, the more creative you will be with a lover. If you have a tendency to go right to the most erogenous zone, try something new. Explore *all* the areas where you're especially sensitive. And remember to practice not being in a hurry. *Take your time.*

Here's another way to experience self-intimacy: explore masturbating while watching in a mirror. You'll want to save this one for when you're feeling good about yourself (or when you're already aroused, which helps to quiet the areas of the brain involved in self-criticism). You might start by putting on something you feel sexy in. As you explore your body, let your eyes be drawn to any aspect of your reflection that is sensual or intriguing in some way. This can be a very personal process that will leave you feeling more connected to your own sexuality.

"Watching myself in a mirror is far more intimate, and even more erotic, than watching someone else in a video," says Kimberly. "The experience stays with me afterward and really helps me appreciate myself as a sexual, desirable woman."

Masturbation as a Meditation

Most people who masturbate typically use some kind of mental or visual stimulation (such as fantasizing, watching erotic videos, or reading sexual material) to speed things up. By turning your mind off once in a while and exploring self-pleasure from a purely physical perspective, you'll become more aware of the sexual energy flowing through your body.

Once you get comfortable and begin to slowly touch and caress yourself, focus your attention on all the different sensations that your body is experiencing. If thoughts or images come in, let them drift by without following or holding on to them and move your attention back to what you're experiencing physically.

Amber says that when she first tried masturbating without fantasizing, "a picture popped up in my head, an image I would typically use to get myself excited, and it was hard to let it go. But when I cleared my mind and went back to the feeling, the orgasm was unbelievable—different from anything I've ever experienced. I felt it in every part of my body. I was very aware of my heart pounding and the blood pumping through me. I really noticed what was happening in my body in a way I haven't before."

> Just being aware of your sexual energy keeps you sexually vibrant.

Several years into her marriage, Brigitte had gotten into the habit of fantasizing every time she and her husband had sex. Practicing turning her mind off while she's masturbating has made it much easier to do so when she and her husband are making love.

"My fantasies were taking me away from the experience we were having together," she says. "Being able to switch them off when I want to makes me feel much more connected to him."

Tonya says that masturbating without a fantasy feels as if she is "opening up and just receiving the pleasure." Barbara finds the practice "softer and more passionate" than using a fantasy. Larry describes the practice this way: "I feel as if I'm surfing into orgasm instead of jumping there with a sexy image." And Jordan says, "It actually feels more sexual when I *don't* fantasize, like the fantasy gets between me and my sexuality."

Another way to make masturbation a meditation is to put your attention on something sensual, such as the flickering flame of a candle, a single flower in a vase, the sound of the wind outside, or the sun streaming in through the window. Or try focusing on just a feeling, like warmth, connection, or love.

Cultivate Sexual Energy by Playing at the Edge of Orgasm

During an orgasm, you experience a release of sexual energy. The ancient practice of delaying orgasm stimulates sexual energy but doesn't discharge it, so it is a way of conserving and cultivating that energy. This increases your libido and your capacity to be sexually aroused, an especially beneficial practice if you've been feeling sexually depleted or uninspired.

Deborah can attest to this: "Getting myself right to the edge of orgasm and playing there makes me feel *alive*." And Kyle says, "After an initial feeling of frustration that comes from interrupting the usual process, I actually experience a surge of energy."

For someone who has difficulty climaxing, letting go of orgasm as a goal can be especially helpful. And, as explored in Chapter 11, "Opening Up to Your Orgasmic Potential," couples can use the practice of building and sustaining their sexual energy to prolong their sexual experiences and deepen their intimacy.

> **Playing at the edge of orgasm is its own reward.**

Learning how to sustain the state of sexual arousal is also helpful for men who want more ejaculation control. By increasing their awareness of the buildup of sexual energy that precedes ejaculation, they will begin to recognize it sooner and be able to intentionally lower their level of arousal.

You can practice cultivating sexual energy through masturbation. Rather than focusing on having an orgasm, just explore sensation, with the intent of sustaining the state of sexual arousal. Pay close attention to the buildup of sexual energy in your body and all the different physical and energetic effects you feel.

For Annette, who's always climaxed very easily, the practice of cultivating her sexual energy by not always masturbating to orgasm has deepened her connection with her own sexuality.

"It's an intense experience with an entirely new quality," she says. "Like having foreplay with myself!"

Exploring your sexuality is essential to keeping your sexual energy alive and flowing. And the more in touch you are with your sexual energy, the more open you will be to new ways of connecting and experiencing pleasure with a lover.

7

Seduction, Intimacy,
and Keeping the Spark Alive

*Meeting someone new, deepening your connection with the person
you're dating, or feeling closer than ever to your long-term partner,
intimacy is essential at every stage of a relationship. Opening up
and allowing yourself to be truly intimate with another person is
what makes real passion not only possible, but sustainable.*

From books on how to get beautiful women into bed or make any
man marry you, to online chat rooms where people share their
"pickup secrets," to weekend seminars that cost hundreds or even
thousands of dollars, seduction is big business. Though there are
scores of different systems and theories, many "seduction experts"
teach tactics that are nothing more than psychological manipulation. Here's what men might be taught in a $3000 three-day seminar
on how to be successful with women:

Start by identifying your first target. Listen in on her conversation
to learn something about her, then approach her and say, "My intuition

is telling me that [make up something related to what you overheard]."
Give her a little attention, then pull back until she demonstrates her
interest (by smiling at you or touching your arm, for instance), and
then reward her with a compliment. Make sure she knows you're willing to walk away: tell her you have only a few minutes because your
friends are waiting for you. Appeal to her desire for romance by saying you felt an instantaneous connection the moment you first saw
her. Make sure to inject some "subliminally seductive" words into the
conversation, which will arouse her desire. And if you do start dating,
always show her you're a guy who's in control: don't return calls or
texts immediately; be unavailable or cancel a date once in a while.

What type of woman would respond to tactics like these? Most
likely one who has self-esteem issues or who is looking for a certain
kind of validation or attention. Seminar attendees might even be
advised to deliberately target women with "LSE" (low self-esteem).

Obviously, mind games like these are pretty shocking, if not downright sleazy. And they certainly aren't the best way to meet someone
if you're interested in something more connected and longer lasting
than a one-night stand. But as you'll see, there are some fundamental
principles taught in these seminars that are worth examining.

EFFORTLESSLY ENGAGE WITH ANYONE

Let's take a closer look at what you're likely to be taught in that
$3000 course—and then adapt those ideas for the purpose of mak-
ing a *real* connection with someone. Anyone—man or woman, gay

or straight, single or in a relationship—can use our version of the techniques taught in the seminar to make an authentic connection with someone. Even though these suggestions are presented in the context of meeting people in person, they apply to online dating as well. Whether online or in person, dating is all about meeting and engaging with people to see if there's any potential for connection.

- *Believe in yourself.* In the seminar, you'll be told to start repeating to yourself something along the lines of "I have everything any woman could wish for" or "Every woman here wants me" before you even step into a place where you might meet someone new. Affirmations can be a great way to build confidence, but they're most effective if they're something you actually believe. So come up with a statement that works for you, like "I'm friendly, intelligent, and have a great sense of humor" or "There are plenty of women here I can connect with."

- *Showcase your best features.* In the seminar, you'll be reminded that you don't have to be a fashion model to be attractive and desirable. Instead you'll be told to identify your best physical features—like your hair, your broad shoulders, your smile—and then focus on them to build your confidence. It's true that focusing on what you like about your body instead of what you don't will help you feel more comfortable. But what may be more important in making a real connection with someone are your *other* qualities. Enlist a friend to help identify your most positive traits: Your sense of humor? The way you tell a story? Your unusual outlook on life? Recognizing these qualities in yourself will naturally bring them out.

- *Start conversations that promote connection.* Much of the seminar's focus will be on basic social skills, like how to start conversations and keep them going. You will be armed with contrived topics for making conversation, like "Last week my friend's girlfriend broke up with him via text; what do you think of that?" But delivering preplanned conversation starters (especially fabricated ones) can feel awkward and sound inauthentic. Instead, practice creating conversation topics that either encourage the sharing of personal stories or offer an opportunity to explore something intriguing together.

Here's an easy way to share a personal story that can spark interesting conversations: simply look around for a painting, photograph, or other object, and share a memory or story that it brings to mind. "That picture reminds me of when I was a kid and . . ." you might begin, or "This rain reminds me of the time . . ." (Don't think too hard about this; your mind is brilliant at making associations like these if you just get out of its way.) In just a sentence or two, you can include enough details to pique your listener's interest and make it easy for them to respond to what you've said. You can use this same idea to encourage other people to share *their* stories: "What does that painting make you think of?" or "What does this song remind you of?"

> When you're truly curious about who someone is, conversation comes naturally.
>
> ❧

To create a space for exploring something intriguing together, just mention something that *you're* intrigued by and see if there's any interest: "Did you hear about that new treatment for . . . ?" or "Last week I saw the most amazing video of . . ." Or ask what excites them, how they got interested in what they're doing, or what their dreams and aspirations are.

If you're a woman who thinks you shouldn't be the one to start a conversation, that you should always wait for a man to approach you, consider that meeting someone you're attracted to can happen much more quickly when *you* take the initiative. Besides, more than a few men around today say they are happy when a woman makes the first move.

- *Recognize receptivity.* In the seminar, you'll be taught to notice when someone is moving closer to you or pulling back from you. This skill is important not so you can *manipulate* them, as promoted in the seminar, but so that you can tune in to and *connect* with them. If someone does seem to be pulling away from you or is obviously showing no interest, don't take it personally. Remember, you're just testing the waters to see who *does* have an interest in getting to know you.

- *Be genuinely interested.* In the seminar, you'll be instructed to demonstrate your interest in a woman by giving her compliments, especially on her clothing, hair, eyes, or voice. If you want to make a real connection, though, don't worry about what to compliment someone on.

> It's easy to be genuinely interested in someone.
> Just ask yourself, "I wonder what the world looks like through their eyes?"

97

Instead, *pay attention and truly listen*. Rather than thinking about what you're going to say next, give her your full attention. And listen for more than just her words; try to get a sense of her experience.

- *Observe the flow of conversation.* In the seminar, you'll be advised to ask a woman questions about herself to keep her talking. If you're after real connection, though, you're better off developing an awareness of how a conversation is flowing. For instance, don't interrupt the flow by making comments that leave the other person nowhere to go next. Rather than "I've never really had an interest in that," try "I'd love to know what interests you about that." Notice how the first response tends to *end* an exchange, while the second tends to *encourage* one. Or instead of "I don't have any pets," try "I don't have any pets now, but when I was a kid I had this great dog that . . ."

- *Get skilled at moving conversations beyond the small-talk stage.* Because it's not personal, small talk doesn't foster a feeling of connection. If you find yourself talking about the weather, the line you're waiting in, or the rising price of apples, shift into something more personal by asking, "Where's the hottest place you've ever been?" "What's the longest line you've ever stood in?" or "What's the most exotic fruit you've ever tried?" And when they answer, remember to really listen.

> There are lots of potential partners out there.
> The point of starting conversations is simply to identify who they might be.

- *Stop focusing on rejection.* In the seminar, you'll be told to concentrate on playing the numbers and not get tripped up when a particular woman (or several) rejects your advances. If you really want to let go of your fear of rejection, though, it helps to understand this: *Feelings of rejection are caused by what you tell yourself when someone doesn't seem to be attracted to you.* Remind yourself that the purpose of introducing yourself to new people is simply to create a space so you can both see if there's any attraction between you. So watch what you're telling yourself. "She's not attracted to me" means "She's not attracted to me," not "I'm not attractive." And if someone isn't interested, for heaven's sake, be gracious and polite anyway. Besides being the right thing to do, she just might have a friend to introduce you to.

> Practice is what takes you from nervous to natural.

Make Your Mind Work *for* You Rather Than *Against* You If you get nervous talking to new people, or to someone in particular, here's why: at some level, you're concerned about what that person might be thinking about you. You might, for example, tell yourself things like "I won't know what to say," "I'll look awkward," or "She'll think I'm a weirdo." To keep your mind otherwise occupied when you approach someone new, assign it the task of discovering something interesting about that person and maybe even learning something new about yourself. This simple practice will keep your mind from cycling through all the usual thoughts that serve only to make you nervous.

Now it's time for you to take all of these tools and practice making conversation with strangers so that it becomes more natural. Yes, it can take some courage, so bring a friend along for support (maybe even a friend of the opposite sex, who might have some great insight). And don't wait until Saturday night. Anytime you're waiting in line, like at the grocery store, is a great time to practice connecting with people. You never know who you might meet. It's estimated that one in three new couples these days met online. This means two out of three still meet the old-fashioned way: in person.

Finally, here is one of the most valuable tips of all, something the seminar leaders probably won't even mention: *Learn to cultivate a love for life*. A passion for life can make connecting with new people much easier, as you'll be genuinely interested in getting to know them and they'll probably be curious to find out just what makes *you* so passionate.

Nothing makes you more attractive than a love for life.

Let Your Intention Speak for You   The next time you notice someone and wonder if there might be a connection between the two of you, try this little experiment. Rather than trying to think of something specific to say, approach the person with a simple intention to create a space for conversation, and just allow any words to come out on their own. You may be surprised to hear yourself saying something that sounds much more natural than anything you could have prepared in advance.

LOOKING FOR MORE THAN
JUST A HOOKUP?

Despite the seduction industry's focus on enticing women into bed, you might find it reassuring to know that, according to research, the majority of singles are interested in a deeply connected, long-term relationship, not a one-night stand. If that's what you're looking for too, remember that this kind of relationship requires two things. First, there's authenticity, or a willingness to be vulnerable and share who *you* are with another person. Second, there's receptivity, which means being open to and accepting of who *someone else* is.

Of course, such a relationship requires finding someone else who's available for real intimacy. But the great thing is, the more receptive and authentic *you* are, the more likely you are to meet that person. That's because you'll be able to easily recognize *their* receptivity and authenticity.

Authenticity and receptivity not only help you connect with someone you've just met; they're also essential for being able to continually *reconnect* with a lover or long-term partner. *Being authentic and receptive keeps the door to intimacy open.*

"VERY ATTRACTIVE, ULTRA FIT, SUCCESSFUL CEO
WITH HIGH IQ SEEKS . . ."

It's well known that dating profiles listing higher incomes (especially in men's profiles) and younger ages (especially in women's profiles) get more views. So do those, both men's and women's, with more youthful-looking photos. But as tempting as it might be to misrepresent your age, occupation, salary, height, or fitness level (or your relationship status!), don't do it. You don't want to start off a new relationship having to figure out when to confess your deception *and* convince your new love interest that you really are trustworthy.

"People are afraid that if they're honest, they'll scare others away," says Matthew, a chiropractor. "But if she can't be truthful about something as simple as her age, my first thought is, 'What's she going to lie about next?'"

Abby agrees. "He told me he had salt-and-pepper hair, so when we met, I just couldn't stop thinking, *Where's the pepper?* It's not that I care if someone has white hair, or even if he's bald, because I don't. I just felt it would be harder to trust him after that."

Aaron, a firefighter, confesses that lying almost backfired on him. "I almost didn't meet my wife," he says, "because at first I didn't post my real age, and she thought I was too young for her!"

Being as authentic as possible (without disclosing identifying information, such as where you work or live) will help you meet people you're truly compatible with. So take another look at your profile. Could it be there's something you're not including because you think it might scare off potential dates—something someone might actually be *looking* for?

"As a single dad, I love the idea of meeting a woman who's already a mom, who's as into her kids as I am into mine," says Gregg, a high school teacher. "So if she doesn't mention children on her profile, I'm not likely to contact her."

If there's something that's a significant part of your life, find a way to mention it—either in your profile or soon into your correspondence with someone new. If you own three large dogs and spend lots of time with them, you might say you "love taking long walks with my German shepherds." Yes, this could scare off potential suitors who can't stand dogs, but that's a *good* thing.

> The more you let your true self shine through, the easier it will be to meet someone who's attracted to the real you.

In addition, give viewers of your profile a look beneath the "surface you." The more authentic you can be, the better sense they can get of you and whether you might be compatible. Consider these lines from an actual dating profile:

> I have an affinity for cats and talking about life with my nine-year-old niece, shun the pretentious, and am something less than a success at small talk. Interested in world cultures, political economy, and community. I enjoy independent and foreign films, but don't really get abstract art (though I'm willing to learn). I like Django Reinhardt and playing frisbee and driving to Delaware just because I've never been there. I would be interested in a woman who is independent in her beliefs, likes herself, and is sympathetic to others. She would probably be more gregarious than me and also wouldn't mind if I left a party for a while to talk to the dog out back.

Notice that this man has revealed something important about himself, something that other people might try to hide: he's somewhat shy and maybe even a bit of a loner. That information is as helpful for readers of his profile who'd respond, "Definitely not my type" as it is for those who'd say, "Oh, he sounds sweet."

Finally, don't let modesty keep you from highlighting all your great qualities—and you *do* have great qualities. Ask a good friend to review your profile for any you might have left out. Recognize that if your friend sees a positive quality in you, it's there—and then find a way to incorporate it into your profile.

DON'T BE LIMITED BY YOUR LIST

If you're single and have made a list—on paper or just in your mind—of what you want in a partner, make sure your list of *ideals* doesn't end up being a list of *limitations*. What if your perfect match is one year out of your specified age range? In an online search, you'd never find them. By locking you in to ideas about who your "perfect partner" is, your list can actually do you a big disservice.

Samantha, a graphic artist in her late twenties, has been searching for her soulmate for seven years. She's tried everything she's heard about to attract him: visualized exactly what she wants, made a list of all the qualities she desires in him, cleared out space in her closet for him, and affirmed to herself daily that he would soon show up. She's grown frustrated that, after so many years, he is still nowhere in sight.

Although Samantha is eager for a relationship, she has almost completely stopped dating. She can't see the point of going out with someone who doesn't match her list closely enough, who obviously isn't "the one." For example, one quality on her list is "speaks

Spanish," so she immediately dismisses any man who doesn't. With that one desire, and given where she happens to live, she's probably reduced the possibility of meeting someone by almost 90 percent.

If you have a list of what you're looking for in a partner, it can be beneficial—and quite insightful—to try and identify the *essence* of each element on your list.

For example, Samantha realized that with "speaks Spanish," she's really seeking someone who is interested in traveling and culture and adventure. Because of her own limited traveling experiences, however, she associates this quality with speaking Spanish. But a man who speaks any other language, or who is interested in exploring other cultures with her and perhaps learning a new language, is just as exciting a prospect to her. Samantha can see that the broader quality "interested in culture, languages, traveling, or adventure" would make meeting a soulmate much easier.

Identifying the essence of each item on your list opens up more possibilities for you. You'll be less likely to quickly dismiss someone who doesn't seem to match everything you're looking for.

"When I first met Lauri, who has super short hair, I wasn't all that attracted to her physically," says Mike, a computer programmer, who'd always had "long hair" on his mental checklist. "But I liked her personality and we had a lot of the same interests. So I decided to go out with her again, even though in the past I would have ended it after the first date. The more I got to know her, the more attractive she became. Now it's hard to remember *not* feeling attracted to her—or to short hair, for that matter!"

Vivian, a real estate agent who has been with her husband, Ethan, for fifteen years, has several single friends who are searching for a relationship like hers. She's seen them make their lists and says, "The whole list thing makes me crazy. Most items on people's lists are completely, utterly irrelevant

When you're receptive to who someone is, it makes you very attractive.

to what will contribute to making a happy life with someone. If I'd been looking for a partner who shared my interests, I have no doubt that I would never have connected with my husband. He doesn't like to dance, hike, take road trips, or go exploring in wild places. For my part, I don't care for poetry, weird sculpture, offbeat music, playing with film, or many of the other things that interest him. But we make each other happy. That's what matters—not whether he has hair I like or if we can go dancing together."

Connect in Five Minutes or Less If you want to practice being authentic and receptive with people you've just met, try a speed-dating event. You'll be given a few minutes to talk with each of several potential dates. Instead of preparing questions and answers in advance, go without an agenda and just let the conversations progress naturally. Also practice turning off the voice in your head that's telling you things like "I won't have anything to say. We probably have nothing in common." If your attempt to let go of anxiety and connect authentically feels like a failure, don't worry—you get to wipe the slate clean and try again in a couple of minutes.

Expanding your ideas of what you're looking for makes you more receptive. And being receptive works wonders when it comes to meeting people you can connect with.

Wyatt, an environmental engineer, has personal experience with this.

"When I've gone out without being receptive to meeting someone new, nobody interesting shows up," he says. "The moment I'm open to others, there are interesting people all over the place."

Being receptive is just as important when you're getting to know someone. With a minimum of judgment, not only will people feel safer opening up to you; you'll also be able to see *them* more clearly. So just notice when judgments come up and do your best to see the person without them.

> Quieting your judgments makes it easier to hear the voice of your intuition.

In addition, getting your judgments out of the way allows you to hear your intuition. When you feel uncomfortable around someone, intuition will help you to know whether it's your own assumptions, insecurities, or fears that are the cause, or whether you're truly sensing that something isn't quite right.

There's one other advantage to receptivity that might be of interest: *receptivity makes people more attractive.* Think of how *you* feel when someone is receptive to you and genuinely interested in your opinions, ideas, or experiences.

Marcie, a single woman in her mid-twenties, puts it simply: "Receptivity is hot!"

DOES THIS MEAN
I HAVE TO BE VULNERABLE?

Yes, it's true. Being authentic—whether it's your first date or your tenth anniversary—might require you to summon some courage and allow yourself to be vulnerable.

By being vulnerable, we mean being willing to let someone else *see* you. If you're always hiding, afraid to reveal your thoughts, feelings, or desires, you will miss out on the sweet satisfaction of opening up with another human being. Allowing someone to see your humanness is what true intimacy is all about.

Consider Stacey and Jared, who have been married a couple of years. In the months leading up to their wedding, Stacey found herself growing more and more anxious about Jared's friendship with an ex-girlfriend.

"They're close, like brother and sister," she says. "I knew in my heart there was nothing going on, but I just couldn't stop worrying about it." The weight of her ungrounded suspicions finally became too much for Stacey to bear. "It took all the courage I had to confess to Jared what I'd been telling myself about his friendship," she says. "I told him I knew it was probably all in my head, but I wanted to check in with him so I could stop obsessing about it. He was completely surprised—he'd had absolutely no idea what was going on for me. I guess I hid it well."

Stacey says that sharing her fears with her fiancé was a very intimate experience.

"He was so incredibly sweet about it and reassured me to no end of his feelings for me. Now I'm so happy that he has this friendship; I can see it's really great for him. And it's such a relief to let go of a burden like that."

When you're feeling reluctant to reveal something about yourself to someone, it helps to take a look at why. Are you getting an intuitive feeling that it wouldn't be safe for you to be vulnerable? Or is it just your *fear* of being vulnerable that's making you hesitate?

Anything we are afraid to face in ourselves or share with others, such as insecurities or unresolved emotions, can get in the way of connecting with a lover. But when we're able to open up and share these hidden feelings, they lose their power over us. This makes it much easier to release or transform them.

KEEPING THE DOOR TO INTIMACY OPEN

Although many relationships start out being a place where people can be intimate, far too often they soon cease to be so. If you've recently met someone, or already have a partner and want to ensure that your relationship continues to be connected—as well as fun, rewarding, and even exciting—make it your goal to follow these practices:

- *Be responsible for your own experience.* Remember that it's your *interpretation* of whatever's happening in your life that creates your *experience* of it. As Madison says, "Even when my husband isn't doing something the way I'd prefer, *I* decide what kind of experience I'm having, not him." Taking responsibility for your experience means you can change it when it's not what you want. Lisa says, "It's empowering for me to know that I have the ability to change my experience. If I'm frustrated in some way, I've learned that that's when I need to ask, *What's a better way for me to approach this?"*

The more responsibility you take for your experience, the more personal power you will have to create the life you want.

- *Know that you can take care of yourself.* We often believe that meeting our physical, psychological, financial, social, and sexual "needs" is our partner's responsibility. We think our partner owes us love, respect, and understanding and is supposed to know how and when to deliver these things. The truth is, you didn't need someone to fulfill these things when you were single. And if your partner leaves, or dies, you *will* be able to take care of yourself. When you know that you can take care of yourself, you can see all of the things your partner does for you as gifts they give freely, rather than as your needs being fulfilled—and you'll feel more loved, more supported, and much happier.

- *Remember that you and your partner are unique, independent human beings.* When we treat each other as guests in our lives, each of us naturally honors the other's right to chart their own course. We give each other the freedom to make our own choices, decisions, and mistakes, and to pursue our own interests. We don't try to control each other's behavior. We support each other's continued growth and evolution, even when it's scary. And we're grateful for whatever time we get to spend together. Even if you're married (perhaps especially if you're married!), remember that you are each there of your own free will. Do your best to accept your partner for who they are. This doesn't mean you agree with all their opinions or behavior. Acceptance simply means you recognize and acknowledge that this is who they are in this moment.

- *Cultivate unconditional trust.* Elena and Brayden, who have been married ten years, claim their relationship is built on mutual trust. To that end, they have an agreement that they can check each other's emails and texts if they're feeling the need. This practice of "trust but verify" is not really about trust at all; it's about control—or, more accurately, the illusion of control. This agreement essentially means Elena and Brayden *don't* trust each other.

By contrast, Jocelyn and Dani have been together for fifteen years. They have weathered a lot, including an affair Dani had several

---

Make It Your Gratitude Reminder Some of us simply have a harder time than others remembering to put the cap on the toothpaste or the socks in the laundry basket. And you probably already know that pestering your partner to remember details like these can do more harm than good. A simple and sweet practice for dissolving small annoyances before they grow into larger annoyances—or worse yet, into resentments—is to turn them into a reminder of all the good things about having this person in your life. Don't laugh—this works! Cap on the counter or socks on the floor? Let that be your reminder to reconnect with your gratitude for this person being in your life. As you get good at this, you might even find yourself disappointed when they *do* remember!

---

years into their relationship. Jocelyn says, "I do trust Dani. Does that mean I trust her to *never* do anything I don't want her to do? No, of course not. I'd rather put my trust in something realistic, something I *can* control: I trust that whatever happens, we'll do our best to learn from it and get back to a connected place."

The kind of trust that Jocelyn is talking about is unconditional. What is unconditional trust? It's trusting that whatever happens in your relationship, you'll find your way through it and learn something you can use going forward. Unconditional trust may seem scary, because we feel as if we're not in control. But rather than making a relationship weak or fragile, it gives it true strength. With unconditional trust, a relationship won't suddenly "break" if the unexpected happens.

- *Be aware of your behavior and motivations.* As often as possible, pay attention to what you're doing and why. Recognize when you have an agenda or when you aren't sharing your complete truth. Notice when you're speaking out of impatience, frustration, or irritation. Be aware of when you're trying to use guilt, anger, withdrawal, or jealousy to manipulate your partner. Notice when you're being critical or judgmental. If you hear yourself complaining, check to see if you're looking for attention, agreement, or validation. Just raising your awareness of what you're doing, and of the motivations behind your behavior, makes it much easier to see what might be preventing you from creating the best relationship possible.

> **One drop of awareness can ripple out in all directions.**

112

- *Keep your relationship as free of expectation, criticism, resentment, jealousy, guilt, and blame as possible.* This sounds like a tall order, we know. But the more of all this that accumulates in our relationships, the less intimacy we'll be able to experience. So look for ways to keep your relationship as free of these dynamics as possible. When something comes up, for example, you might ask yourself these questions: *What opportunity could this give us? How could this actually contribute to our relationship? What is there to appreciate about this being in our lives right now?* In addition, the practice of invitation (see Chapter 9) is a powerful way to not only dissolve things like expectation, resentment, and blame, but to keep them from developing in the first place.*

- *Stay open to your constantly changing partner.* After being in a relationship for a while, we may come to believe we "know" who our partner is, such as what they like and don't like or even what they're thinking or experiencing in a given situation. Eventually we might find it difficult to see them any other way. For example, if you believe that your partner is inflexible, your mind—which is programmed to find evidence for anything you believe—will continually point out all the ways this is true. This makes it unlikely that you'll notice when they're actually being flexible. So watch for any ideas you develop or comments you make about

---

* If a lot of these dynamics have already accumulated in your relationship, you may want to read *The Soulmate Experience: A Practical Guide to Creating Extraordinary Relationships*, which is filled with ideas and techniques for freeing your relationship from these and other "relationship destroyers."

"how" your partner is, and question them. By staying open to really seeing your partner, you create a healthy environment for ongoing intimacy.

WHAT TO DO WHEN YOU (FINALLY) REALIZE YOU CAN'T CHANGE YOUR PARTNER

If you're in a relationship and your partner isn't interested in creating an environment for deep connection and intimacy, it's helpful to remember that you always have three choices. These are the same three choices you have about anything in your relationship that you wish were different.

Choice 1: Continue to respond as you have been. This might involve trying to get your partner to see things your way, getting frustrated, or withdrawing. We may make this choice for years before we come to the understanding that, for now, our partner simply isn't ready to change. Until your partner actually *wants* to change, pressuring him or her to do so will result only in frustration and resentment for both of you.

Choice 2: Leave the relationship. This can be a very difficult decision to make, especially if you've been together for a long time or if there are children involved. Many people don't make this choice until they've spent years struggling to improve their relationship. But it's almost always the best choice for someone who's in an abusive or violent situation or in a relationship that is seriously unhealthy.

If you make the choice to leave, do your best to do so from a place of love and compassion, with everyone's best interests at heart.

Even if your partner is unable to come from a similar place, the transition will be smoother if you can, and even if only some of the time. You'll also accumulate much less negativity this way, making it easier for you to be receptive to and ready for a new relationship when that time comes. And remember, you don't have to go this path alone. There is plenty of help available to you, whether in the form of family, friends, counselors, books, or support groups.

Choice 3: Change your experience. Your third choice, and often the most transformative, is to stay for the time being, but to change your experience. You can do this by consciously choosing to remain in the relationship, for now, while accepting the reality that your partner is unwilling to change, for now. This will free up the energy you've been spending in resistance and allow you to put more energy into all the things you *do* love about your life.

Intimacy is at the heart of every truly connected relationship. It's also the key to creating and sustaining a deeply fulfilling sexual connection with your lover. When you open the door to intimacy, you open the door to lasting love, passion, and desire.

8

Sex and the Practice of Being Present

The more present you and your partner can be with each
other, the more love and intimacy you will both experience.
Knowing how to bring your full attention to making love
will also ensure that your sex life continues to be
exciting, fulfilling, and downright fun.

"I've had my share of relationships, but only one real lover."

Sonya, a freelance writer in her forties, says that many of the men she's known often seem unable to really tune in to a woman.

"It's as though they're not fully there with you," she says.

Sonya talks about some of the signals that men might notice if they were paying more attention.

"Let's say I'm really getting into something my lover is doing," she says. "I'm sighing or moaning, my body is pressing toward him to get closer: the message here is *yes yes yes!* But then if he suddenly stops and moves on to something else, my body's response will be pretty obvious: I'll stop moaning, stop pressing into him. Or if he starts to do something that feels uncomfortable, I might tense up or even pull back from him. But so often guys just don't seem aware of these cues. It's almost as if they're on autopilot."

Why doesn't Sonya just ask for what she wants?

"I'm happy to ask for what I want," she says. "But if I have to ask all the time, it feels like we're not really connected."

How is Sonya's "one real lover" different?

"When we make love, Philip's really *here* with me," she says. "That makes sex much more than just a physical experience."

Theo, a sex therapist, hears stories similar to Sonya's all the time.

"It's the biggest complaint that so many women have," he says. "The minute they start to kiss someone, they're being groped and their shirt's being unbuttoned and their pants are coming off. There's no time spent just being present with each other and enjoying the experience of intimately connecting with someone."

Even women who are easily aroused say that their partners sometimes try to move things along too quickly.

"I actually get turned on and climax very easily," says Victoria, who's also in her forties. "But if you really want me to open up sexually, to become super orgasmic, you've got to listen to my body."

Victoria believes that the rewards of learning to listen to a woman's body are well worth the effort.

"When a man's willing to take the time, to notice my response to his touch, to sense whether my body is pulling away or asking for more—well, we're going to have an incredible experience together."

It's not just women who say their lovers are often not present with them. Cary, who is in his late twenties, has experienced this with some of the women that he's dated.

"When a woman tries to be a 'sex kitten,' acting out what she's seen in movies or what she thinks she's supposed to do," he says, "it's as if I'm watching a performance instead of participating in an intimate experience. It's hard to really connect with her."

Cheryl talks about this dynamic from the perspective of someone who's actually played the "sex kitten" role.

"In college, I hooked up because everyone did; it was just expected," she says. To be able to do this, "I had to close myself off from feeling, because the men I was with didn't really care about me as a person, just as a body. So I'd just shut down and act like I was enjoying it."

After graduating from college and spending a few years not dating at all, Cheryl is now in a new relationship.

"I'm just now starting to learn how to open up to someone," she admits.

To be a great lover, you don't need to be armed with an arsenal of sexual techniques. What you need is to be truly present with the person you're with and the experience you're creating together. When your full attention is on what you're doing and who you're with, you'll be *discovering* new techniques all the time.

The ability to be present heightens every experience you and your lover have together. It's also the best-kept secret for keeping a long-term sexual relationship compelling and alive.

MOVE OUT OF YOUR HEAD TO
GET PRESENT IN BED

The more you're lost in thought while making love, the less connected, and less pleasurable, lovemaking will be. This is true whether
you're being distracted by worries about the future, concerns about
your body, or frustration that the experience you're having isn't living up to your (or your partner's) expectations.

Letting Go of Worry, Anxiety, and Other
Negative Thought Patterns

Some people experience almost nonstop mental distractions during
sex. Darren, who manages a convenience store, admits to this.

"I have rarely been completely involved in the experience," he
says. "In fact, I'm usually about 50 to 70 percent involved—not
entirely disconnected from my partner, but existing in a world of
thought and worry. For me it's *thought thought thought thought* orgasm
thought thought thought. I can only imagine what sex would be like if I
could turn those thoughts off."

Sanford, a financial adviser, confesses to a similar problem.

"I'm wondering if she's enjoying what I'm doing, and she's probably wondering the same about me. Between the two of us we're
probably having a million thoughts. If we could just shut those
voices up, someone could actually have a good time!"

Any time you find yourself distracted from the experience of making love, that's your cue to shift your attention away from your mind
and back into your body. Put your entire focus on all the physical

sensations you're experiencing: the feeling of your lover's body pressed against yours, the support of the mattress or pillows beneath you, the movement of air over your skin. Really take in the scent of your lover's hair, the rhythm of their breathing, the feel and taste of their skin. Can you sense the sexual energy moving between you?

Dropping Thoughts of Inadequacy and Other Self-Criticism

Another very common obstacle to intimacy is self-criticism, such as thoughts of not being "enough."

Hannah, a young mother of two, knows all about this.

"I find it really difficult to get into the moment with my husband while we're making love," she says. "He even tells me, 'I know you think you're twenty pounds overweight, but you're beautiful to me. So let's stop talking about it and just get naked!' The two or three times that I've been able to get out of my head and really be into what's happening, when I stopped thinking about what I look or sound like, it was so much more passionate: a full-on, wholehearted, completely fulfilling experience.

"'I wish you could do that all the time,' he tells me. 'The sex is so incredible.'"

Hannah's husband is pointing to a simple but profound truth: *The more into the experience of making love you are, the more turned on your lover will be.*

Here's another simple truth: *You can't experience all the pleasure your body is capable of when you're being self-critical.*

When Hannah hears that negative voice start up, that could be her reminder to shift her attention from what she imagines her husband is *thinking* about her body to how she is *feeling* in it. By changing her focus, she will experience an almost immediate increase not only in sensation and pleasure, but also in the connection she feels with her husband.

"Those times I let go of worrying about how I look, we really do have a great time together," Hannah says. "Not to mention that my orgasms come so much more easily."

Freeing Yourself from Sexpectations

One more challenge to connecting sexually is having expectations about sex, or what we might call "sexpectations." For example, many people have well-defined ideas of exactly what "having sex" with someone involves. Jeanne, who is nearing eighty, says, "In my world, sex meant intercourse, period."

Expectations around sex—typically acquired from our families and friends, society, the media, or previous relationships—can be so ingrained that we're not even aware of them. Sexpectations can cause us to have a "sexual agenda" and, consciously or not, always be trying to move things in a certain direction. The problem is, when these expectations aren't met, they have the potential to cause disappointment, frustration, anger, and resentment.

> **The more you let go of the idea that "having sex" means anything in particular, the more satisfying your sex life will be.**

"When a man wants more than what's happening right now— when he's thinking, 'How far can I get? When should I make my next move? How can I get her clothes off?'—you can feel that energy, and it's not sexy at all," says Sonya. "On the other hand, if he doesn't get ahead of himself and is really here with me, it gives my body time to respond and open up to him."

Theo, the sex therapist, describes it this way: "Just because you're feeling attracted to someone and they're feeling attracted to you doesn't mean anything in particular has to happen. That kind of thinking can kill intimacy and creativity."

Sexpectations can also manifest as judgments about how the experience you're having compares with ones you've had in the past.

Brenda, who has been married for many years, reflects on this.

"When we have our 'sexometer' turned on and are constantly comparing what's happening now to how it was before, like, 'I think it was better last time,'" she says, "sex just can't be as connecting or satisfying."

So if you find that you're spending your time during sex wondering about what's going to happen next, or comparing what's happening now to some previous experience, or trying to take things in a particular direction, it's time to move your attention back into your body. By just enjoying the physical intimacy of being close, of kissing or caressing, you will learn to let your attraction and sexual energy build naturally. And you'll discover that sexual experiences can be far more powerful, pleasurable, and connecting when you go into them without an agenda.

If you're tempted to ask, "But what about getting my sexual needs met?" consider this: Our true physical needs are food, water, shelter, and anything else that, if we don't have access to it, could potentially threaten our survival. Beyond that, whatever we call a need is, in reality, something we simply want or desire. We tell ourselves that if we don't get these "needs" met, we will experience unhappiness in some form, such as disappointment, frustration, resentment, or anger.

> In the absence of sexpectations, every sexual encounter can be a brand new experience.

There's really no such thing as a sexual need. What we do have is sexual desire: the desire for intimate physical, emotional, and spiritual connection—which we'll be getting a whole lot more of as we let go of our sexpectations. Besides, getting your desires fulfilled sounds far more exciting than having your needs met, don't you think?

Harry has discovered the value of letting go of sexual expectations. "I never used to be able to tell with a woman if I was trying to move

---

Ask Yourself Four Questions Whenever you find yourself distracted while making love, ask yourself these four questions. This quick check-in will bring you into the present and instantly intensify the experience you're having.

- Am I relaxed?
- Am I breathing?
- Am I feeling connected?
- Am I having fun?

things along too fast. I'd get nervous, because I didn't know when to hold her hand or to try to kiss her," he says. "Then I read on a dating site that I should just ask a woman, *Is it okay if I kiss you? May I touch you here?*, but that felt really awkward and disconnecting."

Harry has now learned that "when I just let the physical experience—whether it's a kiss or a touch or anything else—develop naturally instead of trying to force it, I'm much more relaxed than I used to be."

Remember the role of the sex kitten? Someone who is acting out of expectations they have about how they're "supposed" to look, act, or respond may find it challenging to have a truly connected experience. If you recognize that you're performing a sexual act or playing a sexual role solely because you think it's expected of you, slow down a little. Remind yourself to let passion, desire, or love lead you, rather than expectations or insecurities. Not only are you likely to have a better experience, you might also discover that your real, authentic responses are just as exciting to your lover as anything you could fake (and probably more so!).

PRESENCE: THE REAL SECRET TO KEEPING LIFE IN YOUR SEX LIFE

Yes, it is absolutely possible many years into a relationship to still be able to say, "We have a great sex life. It never feels the same." The following ideas will help you and your lover keep the life in your sex life:

- *See each other through new eyes.* When you first start dating someone, you're asking the question *Who are you?* all the time. After a while,

it's not uncommon to stop asking that question. But no matter how long you've been
together, neither of you is exactly the same
person you were a year ago, or even a week
ago. So practice seeing each other with
openness and receptivity while letting go of
any beliefs, ideas, or judgments you might
be holding, along with any mental chatter

> Being open and
> receptive to
> who each other is
> in this moment
> creates space for
> new experiences
> to unfold.

about what you're seeing. Your lover might appear to transform
right before your eyes. Rob, a graphic designer, practices this with
his girlfriend. "Although we have this history together," he says,
"there's always something new to see when we really look. It creates this whole excitement." You might also imagine that you've
just met and try kissing or making love as if for the very first time.

- *Be willing to take a risk.* A willingness to try something different,
  to experience something new, is one of the easiest ways to keep
  your sex life vibrant. As Sue, who is just turning sixty, puts it,
  "When you both know what the other likes, sex can get very routine. It's okay to try some crazy stuff once in a while and decide,
  'Well, *that* didn't work!' Just getting creative together is what keeps
  you connected." Taking a risk might also mean allowing yourself to be vulnerable, like being willing to share a secret fantasy
  or desire with your lover. "My husband and I often explore new
  and creative ideas to spice up our bedroom activities," says Jess.
  "While this can be awkward at first, those feelings quickly turn
  into excitement and anticipation of what might happen next."

- *Take time to indulge in each other.* When we've been together awhile, it's not uncommon for our sex life to become predictable. One working mother puts it this way: "We're so in the mode of *do do do* all the time that it can be challenging to slow down, relax, and just *be* with each other." So take any opportunity to unwind and allow all the other stuff to drop away for a while. Explore. Get sensual. Be creative and playful.

Kirstie and Derek, who have been together eighteen years and have two children, know all about taking time and space to really be with each other. "Complacency is the main evil in every relationship," Derek acknowledges. "When it gets really routine, a sexual relationship can become mundane; it's just having sex. When it starts to get boring, Kirstie says so immediately: 'Stop. Freeze. We've got to do something!'"

"It's good to go somewhere different, away from your environment, your phone, your email," Kirstie says. "When we're away from all of that, a playfulness comes out. A new venue helps us to let go and ask, 'Who are we *now?*' When we come back, we're a bit more 'switched on'; we're feeling more passionate and connected."

Even if you don't have the luxury of getting away for a night or a weekend together, you can still indulge in each other. How about enjoying a warm shower together, offering each other a foot massage, or getting lost in a passionate thirty-second kiss?

Being lovers is about continually exploring new ways to connect.

- *Focus on quality, not quantity.* The frequency with which you have sex is not the best measure of the health of your sexual relationship. The quality of your encounters, and the connection and pleasure you experience through them, is a much better indicator. Meredith and Kate, for

> **When you have the time, go beyond just making a sex date— squeeze in an entire sex weekend!**

example, are both busy executives who travel a lot. Although they have sex only about once a month, they say, "It's enough for us, because it's always intimate, connecting, and very passionate."

- *Make love for no reason.* When's the last time you lost track of time while making love? For many couples who have been together

---

Create a Sexual Intention Setting an intention for a sexual encounter—an intention designed for deepening your intimacy—can help you to be more present. For example,

- If you tend to be worried or anxious, you might try out this intention: "Tonight I'm going to relax and just have fun."
- If you're always more comfortable as the giver than as the receiver, try: "I'm here to enjoy all the sensations flowing through my body."

You can also create an intention together. For example,

- After a stressful week: "Our intention tonight is to just let go and enjoy ourselves."
- After spending time apart: "Our intention for this experience is to relax and reconnect."
- When your sexual energy is high: "Our intention is to provide each other with as much pleasure as possible."

---

awhile, sex can eventually seem to become nothing more than a "race for an orgasm." Make love with an open mind and free of any expectations. "When you don't have the idea that sex has to progress in a certain way," says Troy, who has been married several years, "it's a constant exploration: sexually, physically, and even spiritually." With your only objective for making love being to enjoy the exploration, you'll be discovering a whole new world of pleasure together.

- *Don't miss out on the love.* Sometimes we think our partner isn't giving us enough affection, when the truth is that we just haven't been paying enough attention.

Suppose that when Kim and Dan first meet, he puts his arm around her whenever they walk together. She loves this and tells him so regularly. After a while, though she still enjoys it, she stops telling him as often. Dan, with less feedback, begins to do it less often. Kim, feeling he isn't showing her as much affection as he used to, starts to feel down when they walk together. Dan, sensing the change in Kim's mood, tries to give her more space. Can you see where this is headed? If you recognize yourself here—on either side—know that this is perfectly normal human behavior. It just doesn't necessarily make for a connected experience.

> Just touching fingers, even after many years, is a delicious feeling when you're really paying attention.

If you feel you don't get enough love or attention from your partner, make sure that any time your partner does give you their

129

attention, whether that's a hug, a kiss, a smile, a simple touch, or a compliment, you let everything else go for a moment and really take it in. You may be surprised to find that the love and attention you feel you're receiving suddenly increases tremendously.

- *Tap into the power of appreciation.* By grasping the truth that the person you love won't be here forever—that you could lose them in an instant, with no warning and no opportunity to say goodbye—you tap into a source of tremendous gratitude. Understanding that it's not a question of *if* your relationship will someday change, but of *when*, makes you much more appreciative of what you have right now.

> Gratitude makes your relationship, and your life, a whole lot sweeter.

SENSUAL MASSAGE: THE PERFECT WAY TO PRACTICE BEING PRESENT TOGETHER

Erika, a massage therapist and sex educator, teaches the importance of learning to speak the language of touch.

"Imagine that you're speaking with your hands," she says. "What are they saying? If you're not paying attention to how you're touching, if you're not using your hands and your intuition to listen to what's being said back to you, there's an entire conversation going on that you're just not aware of."

Giving each other sensual massages is a wonderful way to practice touching with "care and consciousness," as Erika encourages the couples she works with to do. Erika also points out that in long-term relationships, we can sometimes forget about "touching with the intention to turn on." All the more reason to treat each other to a sensual massage.

Read through the possibilities that follow, which you can adapt in any way you like, to get a sense of what sensual massage is all about. Then make a date with your lover and let your hands and your heart be your guide. (Although the focus here is on a woman, these ideas can just as easily be applied to a man.)

> The more fluently you speak "touch," the more pleasurable touching will be.

Gather some soft sheets and blankets, a couple of pillows, natural oil or lotion (having options is a nice touch), a glass of water, and maybe a few sweet-smelling flowers. Prepare a firm but comfortable surface to lie on; you might even see if you can borrow a massage table from a friend. Make the space intimate: warm up the room, put on some soft music, light a candle or two. Get yourself in the mood by slipping into something that feels comfortably sensual.

Welcome your lover into the space you've created. Even if you've seen her naked a thousand times before, add a little romance by stepping out for a few minutes. Give her this time to undress and get settled on her stomach under a light blanket or sheet.

When you enter the room, ask if there's anything you can do to make her more comfortable, such as placing a pillow under her stomach, hips, or feet. Rub a drop of each oil or lotion into her skin to see if she has a preference.

Take a moment to connect. Help her relax by saying something like "For the next hour or so, there's nothing you need to do but let go and open up to the pleasure of being touched. If something doesn't feel just right, guide me to what does. If something feels especially good, I'd love to know."

Ask if there are any areas that need care, love, or special attention. If the two of you have a close and loving connection, you might let her know that anything that comes up for her—emotions, fears, desires, passion—is okay to experience and express here.

What you're doing through all of this is creating a space that feels safe, both physically and emotionally.

Start by gently running your hands over the length of her body, just so she knows you're there. Move slowly, which signals to her that it's okay to relax and let go.

Once you've awakened her senses, pull the sheet aside to reveal just the first area of her body that will be receiving your love and attention. Move slowly, pressing softly into her skin, exploring every inch with a very gentle touch. When you feel it's time, start to play with longer, firmer strokes that use a little more pressure. To really entice her body to relax, spend some extra time massaging oil or lotion into any muscles that feel tense or tight. When it's time to move on to a new area of her body, gently re-cover the first before uncovering the next.

All the while, encourage your lover's trust in your touch by listening to her body's responses. Pay attention to the rhythm of her breathing. Is she sighing or moaning? Notice whether her muscles are relaxing beneath your hands. Can you feel her letting go? When you discover something she particularly enjoys, *indulge her.*

You never know what experiencing a sensual massage might bring up—an emotion, a memory, a physical reaction. If this happens, just quietly being there for her is almost always the best thing you can do.

Before asking her to turn over, spend some time concentrating on the region from her upper thighs to her lower back, including her butt cheeks. Using firm, smooth strokes, slowly massage oil or lotion into the entire area. Then, focusing on one side at a time, rhythmically squeeze and massage all the muscles in her hip, lower back, cheek, and upper thigh. Use your fingertips to explore an area more deeply and your palms to apply broader pressure. And don't be shy about checking in to see if there is any place where she'd like a little extra attention.

The butt cheeks and the insides of the upper thighs can be very erotic regions to explore through touch, and most massages don't include them. But in a sensual massage, you want to explore the sensual potential of the entire body, and that most certainly includes the erogenous zones.

> Listen for your lover's response when giving a sensual massage. If she starts to moan, you're doing just fine!

When it feels right, invite her to turn onto her back. Start as you did before, lightly running your fingers over her body from her face to her toes. Then begin an exploration with the intention of arousing her. Using her responses and your own intuition as your guides,

133

start to focus on erogenous zones like her neck and ears, her hips, and her inner thighs, inviting her body to open up to you.

When you turn your attention to her breasts, resist the temptation to go straight for the nipples. Instead, take your time with the rest of the breasts: the sides, the upper chest, the sometimes-overlooked undersides. Many women find it very sensual, and sexy, to have their entire breasts lovingly held and massaged—especially if they've been strapped into a bra all week long. When you begin to explore her nipples, keep in mind that they can be especially sensitive. Start gently and let her responses direct you.

When it feels right to move your loving touch to her genital area, remember this: *Your goal is not necessarily to bring your lover to orgasm, but simply to be present with her and help her experience as much sensuality, pleasure, and connection as possible.* You might remind her that you're here to please her and that she's welcome to guide you at any time.

As with her breasts, don't start with the most sensitive areas. Instead, help her to relax and open up to you, while building sensation and anticipation, by slowly moving your way toward those areas. Although you can find a lot of sexual techniques in books or online, every woman is different, and every sexual encounter is new. Look for any signs that she's getting turned on: a moan, a sigh, a flush over her face or chest, a change in the rhythm of her breath, swelling of her nipples or vulva. Pay attention to her excitement level as you play with stroking, teasing, and caressing her. When you're really present and tuned in to her, you'll easily discover just what kinds of touch, in this moment, will bring her the most pleasure.

A sweet finishing touch to a sensual massage is to just lovingly hold her, for as long as she'd like to be held.

Adrian and Sasha, who have been in a long-distance relationship for many years, say treating each other to sensual massages "is a sweet, romantic, and erotic way to reconnect with one another. It feels like we're rediscovering our bodies and what they can experience together."

If this little adventure into the realm of sexual massage has put you in the mood, you might want to just enjoy that feeling for awhile before reading on.

PORNOGRAPHY ADDICTION AND ITS EFFECT ON PRESENCE

As unsexy as the topic is, an exploration of sex and presence wouldn't be complete without a mention of pornography addiction. Some people strongly believe that all pornography is damaging, while others just as strongly believe that some types of pornography, used with awareness, can be a healthy aspect of sexuality. However you may personally feel, everyone would probably agree that an *addiction* to pornography can greatly affect a person's ability to be present with a lover.

Watching pornography has measurable effects, both on the brain and on the body's hormone levels. Pornography addiction has been linked to increased infidelity, more unhappiness in one's relationship, and a higher rate of divorce. In addition, it is almost certainly a contributor to the recent increase in impotence among young men and is associated with the rising rate of sexual assault on college campuses.

Overconsumption of pornography can lead to less interest in a real-life lover. If you associate orgasms with your lover's scent, skin, touch, or personality, that is what will turn you on. If you associate orgasms with a certain type of pornographic imagery, *that's* what it will take to turn you on.

Lindsay, a hair stylist, has personal experience with this.

"My last boyfriend was interested in sex with me only if I did things in a very specific way," she says. "The way he watched them done online."

Another problem is that most pornography, especially mainstream pornography, offers a very limited perspective on sexuality.

Abigail, a sex educator, is concerned about what effects this is having on people, especially young men.

"Video porn offers them a very narrow picture of sexuality," she explains. "Many of them learn that if they put their penis into a woman in any way and squeeze her breasts a few times, she will have an orgasm. What's missing from this 'education' are things like where are a woman's *other* erogenous zones? How do you tell if a woman is turned on? How do you listen to her body so you can be the best lover possible?"

Theo, the sex therapist, has similar concerns.

"Far too many young people are learning about sexuality from mainstream porn, and it's not healthy sexuality by any means. They're learning that if it doesn't have penetration and orgasm, it's not a 'good scene.' Pornography has wired us to look for these things, and if our own sexual experiences fall short of them, we consider those experiences unsuccessful. Mainstream porn devalues the subtleties of sexuality and sends the message that if you don't go all the way, then it's not worth doing at all."

Adam, a psychiatrist who specializes in the treatment of depression, says he frequently counsels men who believe they are sexually inadequate because of the size of their penis. His patients are usually quite shocked when Adam tells them what the average size of a man's penis really is. Their distorted impression, of course, comes from comparing themselves to the men they watch on screen (who are chosen specifically because of their much-larger-than-average size) and deciding they just don't measure up.

Two men who have struggled with pornography addiction have their own insights to share.

Randall is currently recovering from a decades-long addiction that destroyed his career and made intimate relationships next to impossible. What does he think the most damaging aspect of pornography is?

"Porn is totally lacking in intimacy," he says. "Real intimacy can occur only between real people. And real intimacy is where life's real pleasure is."

Dmitri is a young man who started watching pornography regularly as a high school senior and was consumed by it in college.

"The more I watched, the less aroused I would get," he confesses. "There were times in college where I would waste an entire day sitting in front of the computer watching porn. And I still always needed more, more intensity. I think that's why there's so much violence in it."

Both Randall and Dmitri stress that *pornography addiction is a real addiction*. And, like any addiction, it can be difficult to kick. Especially because this "drug" is available twenty-four hours a day, seven days a week, almost anywhere you are, and you can almost always get it for free.

This constant search for "more"—whether more violence, more graphic visuals, more extreme scenarios, more sex partners, or younger and younger participants—drains a person's energy, including their sexual energy. Dmitri, in fact, was so depleted by his pornography addiction that he dropped out of college.

After joining a group for sex addicts in recovery, Dmitri has been pornography-free for two years and is just now learning how "to be in a real relationship."

If you are a regular viewer of pornography, watch for any negative effects it might be having on you. Is it causing you to feel insecure, isolated, pessimistic, aggressive, or even depressed? Are you becoming desensitized, needing more and more while feeling less and less? If your answer to either question is yes, you might want to take a break for a while and see what effect that has.

"I am drained after watching most porn," says Jayne, a successful romance novelist. "It feels like it takes something *from* me instead of giving something *to* me. Now the only kind that holds any interest for me is when I can sense a real connection between the actors."

Everything we try to get from pornography—anticipation, pleasure, connection—we can experience with a real-life lover when we're present with them.

Theo advises his clients who do choose to view pornography, whether by themselves or with a lover, to be conscious about what they watch.

"I'm not against pornography as a concept," he explains. "There are ways of filming really healthy and loving sexuality that are still considered pornography but are not the mainstream. If you, or you and your partner together, want to explore erotic video, look for high-quality erotica that focuses on connection and sensuality rather than on close-ups and degrading or violent scenes."

What's different about the "high-quality erotica" that Theo is referring to? For one, the people involved in making the films, who are very often women, approach erotica as a sensual art form. Their films feature themes that are more creative, genuine, and respectful than those in mainstream pornography, and the actors seem to be experiencing real passion and pleasure. What's different about these films, in essence, is that the filmmakers and the actors are more *present* with what they are creating together.

The more presence you can bring to your love life, the more exciting and fulfilling your love life will be. In fact, it could be said that presence is your magic ticket for continually experiencing great sex.

9

The Power of Invitation

When it comes to relationships, invitation is the number one
secret for having it all: getting your desires fulfilled while
simultaneously increasing the love and intimacy between you
and your partner. In fact, the art of invitation may end up being
the most versatile and valuable skill you'll ever have—not only
in your relationships, but in the rest of your life as well.

Teresa and Dillon, who belong to the same photography group, were friends for several years before getting romantically involved. When they finally began going out, things progressed quickly and it wasn't long before they were talking about a possible future together. Everything was a huge *yes* for Teresa, except for one minor thing: Dillon turned out to be much less sexually assertive than she'd always imagined he would be.

"I'd seen his take-charge side from time to time before we started dating," she says, "and imagined how exciting that would be in the bedroom. But he's always very loving and gentle with me, which is great—it's just that once in a while I'd love to be, well, just *taken*."

One day she finally got up the courage to ask him about it.

"I know this is going to sound cliché, but he said he loves me so much he'd never think of treating me as anything but a princess," she says. "His explanation was really pretty sweet. But I still wanted to experience that strong, masculine side of him too."

A few weeks later, before they left on a weekend trip, Teresa secretly went shopping. That Saturday, after spending the day taking pictures of the local scenery, they returned to the cabin they'd rented. While Dillon made a fire, Teresa disappeared into the shower to get herself ready for the surprise she had been planning.

The warm water relaxed her body, and she could feel her anticipation building. She began to imagine herself in the role of an experienced seductress: a woman who was sensual and self-assured, a woman who could entice her lover in endless ways. She watched as that woman in the mirror dried her hair, rubbed lotion over her entire body, and then got dressed in the black lace-up bodysuit she had packed away.

"I love that you think of me as your princess," she said to a stunned Dillon as she walked into the room. "But tonight, I want to be your *bad* princess."

What Teresa was offering Dillon was an invitation: an invitation to get more intimate by bringing out sides of themselves that they hadn't explored together before.

And what if Dillon had been reluctant to play along?

"I went in knowing that was a possibility," Teresa says. "But Dillon and I have been able to work through anything that comes up between us, so I felt okay taking that risk."

Invitation is useful for more than just encouraging your partner to be a little adventurous. It can help you ask for many of the things you might desire in your relationship, and in a way that can actually inspire more intimacy and love.

HOW WE USUALLY TRY TO GET WHAT WE WANT (WHEN ASKING POLITELY DOESN'T WORK)

Below is a list of approaches we often use in our attempts to get what we want in our relationships. Having picked up these tactics from family, friends, the media, and previous relationships, most of us have tried many of them at one time or another.

Spend a few minutes reflecting back on your own relationships. See if you can think of a few instances when you used one or more of these tactics with someone you loved:

- Complaining
- Guilt tripping
- Getting annoyed or frustrated
- Criticizing
- Making demands
- Using sarcasm
- Blaming or making accusations

- Getting angry

- Taking away your love, affection, or attention

We might also add "having expectations" to this list. Holding expectations that your partner "should" do certain things can lead you to use any of the other tactics that are listed.

Now, for each example you identified, consider how well that approach actually worked. Think about not only whether you got what you wanted, but the overall effect the approach had. Did everyone involved feel good about the interaction and the outcome, or did it cause disagreements or disharmony? Did your partner end up feeling guilty, unappreciated, or inadequate? If you didn't get what you were after, were you left feeling frustrated, sad, or even resentful?

Notice that all of the tactics on the list have something in common: they are all forms of manipulation. These behaviors can be so ingrained in us that we may hardly be aware we're using them. Whether we know we're using them or not, they are still manipulation; they may just be *unconscious* manipulation.

Most of us don't enjoy being manipulated, so it's human nature for your partner to respond to such tactics with resistance, such as by getting annoyed, becoming defensive, or ignoring you. And even if the tactics do happen to work, your partner still might end up feeling irritated and resentful.

> **A heartfelt invitation is far more likely to get an enthusiastic yes! than manipulation ever will.**

The point is, *manipulative tactics might get you what you're after in the short term, but they won't produce a connected, fulfilling relationship in the long term.*

A MUCH MORE EFFECTIVE—AND LOVING—WAY TO GET WHAT YOU WANT

Using invitation instead of manipulation is a better choice for several reasons: First, if your partner doesn't feel pressure coming from you, he or she is more likely to consider your proposal in a positive light and feel better about saying yes. Second, with a genuine invitation, you won't be left feeling frustrated, hurt, or disappointed if the answer doesn't happen to be yes. And third, it's much easier for love to thrive in an environment that's free of manipulation.

To harness the power of invitation, follow these three steps:

Step 1: Notice When You're Using Manipulation—and Then Stop

You can't use invitation at the same time as manipulation. So recognizing when you're using manipulation, or are about to use it, is essential.

For example, we often try to hide our true intention behind our choice of words. Suppose Alan really wants his girlfriend, Alexandria, to accompany him to his uncle's house for a family dinner. In an effort to convince her, he might indirectly accuse her of not being committed to the relationship by saying something like "People who are together should show their commitment to the relationship by spending time with each other's family." Or, "If you really loved me, you would *want* to go to this dinner with me." Can't you just feel the guilt trip?

To learn to recognize when you're using manipulation, pay attention when you and your partner have a difference of opinion or are trying to make an important decision together. Listen not only to *what* you're saying but to *how* you're saying it: your tone of voice and the words you choose.

When you catch yourself attempting to use manipulation, one way to make a shift is by actually pointing out your own behavior. If Alan recognizes that he's trying to manipulate Alexandria into going with him, he could get honest with her about what he's noticing: "Wow, did you hear how I was trying to guilt-trip you just now? I don't want to do that. If you go with me, I want it to be because you really want to, not because I pressured you into it." You will probably find that acknowledging what you're doing and admitting it to your partner can instantly lighten the mood and reconnect you with the love you feel for each other.

When you're not using manipulation, you have an opportunity to approach the situation in an entirely different way.

Step 2: Let Go of Your Attachment to the Outcome

The next step to trying invitation is letting go, as much as possible, of any attachment you have to getting what you are asking for.

Carmen, who's been learning the art of invitation, speaks for many of us when she says, "That step is the hardest!" Yes, letting go of our attachment to an outcome can seem quite challenging at first. But when you try it out and are successful a few times, it becomes much easier.

What does it mean to be attached to an outcome? When you are attached to a particular outcome and events don't turn out the way you want, you'll experience some form of unhappiness, like irritation, frustration, or resentment. The less attached you are to the outcome, the better you're going to feel no matter what happens.

Manipulation: Getting what you want by making your partner feel bad.

Invitation: Getting what you want by making your partner feel good.

In Alan's case, if he's attached to the idea of Alexandria accompanying him to his uncle's and she doesn't want to go, he's likely to feel hurt, sad, or disappointed. If he can let go of his attachment to this idea and have it be just a preference—something he'd love to have happen but not something he'll be upset about if it doesn't—he can enjoy himself whether she accompanies him or not.

How do you let go of attachment? Often just remembering that not being attached is an option can help you turn your attachment into a simple preference. And when you hold something as a

---

Make Your Heart Grow Fonder Being apart from the one you love can sometimes be challenging. If you're feeling disappointed because you're going solo to a party, sad because circumstances are preventing you from being together, or lonely because you're just missing your lover's company, use that time apart to reconnect with your love for them and your gratitude for having them in your life. This practice will dissolve feelings of sadness, frustration, and resentment by moving you away from the "bitter" side of bittersweet and toward the "sweet" side!

---

preference, you won't get upset if it isn't met. Here are a few other ways you might be able to make the switch from attachment to preference:

- *Remind yourself that your partner is a unique, independent human being.* He or she is here of their own free will and has the freedom to make his or her own choices, decisions, and mistakes.

- *Take full responsibility for your own happiness.* Let go of the idea that anything in particular has to happen in order for you to be happy.

- *Be genuinely open to seeing things from your partner's perspective.* Acknowledge and accept that this is how your partner feels in this moment.

- *Know that however your partner responds to your request is not a reflection of your value.* Your value—your worth as a person—is intrinsic; it does not depend on anyone else. "No" means that, for now, your partner just doesn't happen to be interested in your offer, not that you're not good enough.

- *Be open to the possibility that not getting what you want in this situation could result in unexpected benefits or opportunities.* This realization makes it easier to let go of your attachment and to see those benefits and opportunities when they do show up.

- *Understand that even if you don't get what you want, invitation will likely have much better consequences for your relationship than manipulation or demands ever will.*

Letting go of an attachment can be challenging. So don't expect yourself to be able to use invitation in every situation. There will probably be outcomes you're not willing to let go of your attachment to—at least not yet.

Step 3: Offer a Genuine Invitation

Beneath (sometimes far beneath) almost every attempt to manipulate your partner is a sincere, authentic desire to connect with the person you love. As you let go of your attachment to a particular outcome, you'll be able to express that desire in a simple, heartfelt invitation.

In Alan's situation, as he lets go of the idea that Alexandria "should" go with him to his uncle's house or that he "needs" her to go, he can get in touch with his authentic desire, which might be something like "I really love being with her." He can then express that desire through an invitation: "Would you like to go to my uncle's house for dinner Saturday night? I really love hanging out with you, and I'd like everyone to see what an amazing woman I have in my life."

When you offer someone an invitation, there's always the possibility that they may be reluctant or even say no. If their response bothers you, that just means you are still carrying some attachment to the outcome. Remind yourself that a true invitation doesn't seek to manipulate, restrict, or control in any way; the other person has the freedom to accept or decline, without pressure, judgment, or repercussions.

> A true invitation is free of obligation. It has no "should" quality to it.

Also, having no attachment doesn't mean saying the right words to give the *appearance* that you have no attachment. That's simply more manipulation. Have you ever said "It's fine" when it wasn't fine at all?

No matter how freely you offer something, of course, it may be that your partner is simply not going to be interested (this time). Or you might be asking for something that's just not negotiable for them, such as moving to a foreign country or having a threesome. When you recognize that the issue in question is non-negotiable, you have a number of options:

- You can keep trying, sometimes for years, to convince your partner to change his or her mind, and never succeed. (Remember, this is non-negotiable for them.)

- You can decide that this issue is so important to one or both of you that the best thing to do is to separate, ideally with as much love as possible.

- You can consider whether there might be some unique, creative approach to the situation that will get each of you much of what you desire, even if it's in a different way from what you originally pictured.

Although invitation is not a guarantee, it's by far a better choice than manipulation, not only for its short-term benefits, but also for the ongoing health and happiness of your relationship. So let's look at how it works. The more examples you see, the easier it will be for you to apply the power of invitation in your own life.

Manipulation comes from the head. Invitation comes from the heart.

USING INVITATION TO
DEEPEN YOUR CONNECTION

When Carmen and Jeremy first started dating, Jeremy made it clear that because he had recently ended a twelve-year marriage, he wasn't ready to get serious anytime soon.

Carmen really liked Jeremy and saw the possibility for a truly amazing relationship, but she was cautious. She never suggested anything for them to do together; instead, she always waited for him to contact her. After a date, sometimes days or even a couple of weeks would go by before Jeremy would reach out again. When he did try to get in touch, she sometimes made it a point not to return his texts or calls too quickly so that he wouldn't know how available and interested she really was.

After almost a year of being hesitant to "put myself out there and face the rejection of having him possibly pull away," she says, "I'd had just about enough. I felt like I was living my life on restriction."

Carmen could see that her reluctance to ask Jeremy out or to let him know how she really felt about him was not getting her what she authentically desired: an opportunity for the two of them to get closer and see where their connection might take them. The only way they would ever be likely to get that opportunity, she realized, was if she did the inviting.

So how did Carmen get past the idea that Jeremy turning down an invitation from her would be a rejection? How did she stop worrying about whether or not he would say yes?

To begin with, she recognized that not being attached to Jeremy saying yes was a real possibility for her. She decided that if he said no, it would mean he wasn't interested, not that she wasn't exciting enough to be with. And she realized that if their relationship ended, she would be sad for a while, but eventually she would go out and "meet someone else to create a really great relationship with."

Letting go of her attachment to Jeremy saying yes made it possible for Carmen to simply invite him to get together. She then found it much easier to make simple offers like these: "A friend has extra tickets to the music festival this weekend; would you like to go with me? It'd be fun to check it out together." "Would you like to come over? My garden is producing like crazy right now and I'd love to make you dinner." Or just "Would you like to do something together this weekend?"

Just as Carmen learned she could invite the person she's dating to explore their connection more deeply, invitation can also be used with someone you've recently met who may not realize they are ready for and capable of having a deeply connected relationship, or who doesn't know that type of relationship is even a possibility. And it's by far the most effective way to encourage a long-term partner to experience more intimacy. When you invite someone to take your connection to the next level—with openness, sincerity, and no attachment to whether they take you up on it—at the very least, they're likely to be intrigued!

> Invitation creates an environment that encourages your partner's willing participation.

152

ASKING AS IF FOR THE FIRST TIME

Whenever she and her boyfriend start to make love, Elaine often finds herself frustrated. Antonio absolutely adores her body, but in his excitement he always seems to forget that it takes her a while to get warmed up. In particular, Elaine's nipples are extremely sensitive, but all too often, Antonio heads straight for them. Elaine pulls away, saying something like "Ouch! I wish you could remember to be more gentle."

She finally had an honest conversation with him about it—and learned something important.

"I'd do anything for you—I'm crazy about you," Antonio assured her. "But I guess I'm not as good at remembering things as I'd like to be. Feel free to remind me any time you're thinking about it."

The fact is, everyone's memory works a little differently. Expecting our partner to remember something that they consistently forget can often lead to frustration, exasperation, or blame. If Elaine succeeds in learning how to ask Antonio for a gentler touch—and asking every time as if it's the first time—she will be able to relax, he will be grateful, and they'll both feel much more sexually connected. (And Elaine, by the way, will pretty much have mastered the art of invitation!)

> Instead of expecting your partner to remember what you like, use invitation to help them rediscover what you like.
>
> ༅

To help you get the hang of this skill, here are some more examples of offering an invitation as if for the first time:

- Instead of "I wish you'd go out on the boat with me once in a while; I'll be taking it out again tomorrow," try "I'd really love to show you the sunset from out on the water tomorrow night; it should be gorgeous."

- Instead of "This is the third time Taylor and Jamie have invited us over for dinner. Am I supposed to just keep going by myself?" try "Taylor and Jamie invited us over for dinner Friday night. Would you like to come? I know you'd love the view from their place, and Taylor is an awesome cook."

- Instead of "I know you don't really like parties, so you probably wouldn't be interested in going to this one with me, would you?" try "If you'll be my date to this party, I promise to wear that blue dress you love so much—yeah, *that* one!"

If you're thinking that any or all of these alternatives could sound manipulative, you're right; almost *anything* can sound that way if it's said with an intent to manipulate. And if it is, you will both feel it. So imagine how each of these examples might sound as a truly genuine invitation, said with no attachment to the outcome and no attempt to manipulate. There's a big difference between trying to convince someone to do something they don't want to do and simply offering them a possibility for why they just might enjoy doing it.

The secret to these kinds of invitations is this: each time you ask, let go of any resentment you might have from when you've asked before, as well as any expectation you might have about the answer this time, and ask as if you were asking for the *first* time. Like any skill, the more you practice this, the easier it will become.

INVITING YOUR LOVER TO FULFILL
A FANTASY OR DESIRE

Invitation may be the best way to entice your lover to try something new, whether that's one of the many explorations in this book or another one you come up with on your own.

Elizabeth, an accountant, tells the story of a fantasy she's had for many years. She imagines herself and her lover arriving separately at an exclusive nightclub. She gets there first and has enough time before he arrives to meet and have a conversation with a couple of gentlemen at the bar. When her lover enters the club, they don't let on that they know each other. She watches him as he orders something to drink. They begin to flirt with their eyes. They move closer. The magnetic attraction between them is undeniable. They leave together— and everyone in the place knows exactly where they're headed.

When she started dating Steve, Elizabeth kept imagining him in the role of her lover in this scenario. "Steve's pretty adventurous in other ways, so I thought he might be open to playing this out with me," she says. "What really enticed him to try it, though, was when I said I loved the idea of everyone there knowing how hot I think he is." Now *there's* a sexy invitation.

Invitation is like holding the door open to a new possibility.

The night of their rendezvous, they drove to a popular bar in an upscale hotel. The plan was that Elizabeth would go in first; Steve would follow in twenty minutes or so. But as soon as Elizabeth opened the car door, Steve panicked. He offered no explanation; he just said he couldn't go through with it.

Elizabeth could have let herself get discouraged or disappointed when Steve backed out, or she could have felt too awkward or embarrassed to ever bring it up again. She didn't do any of those things, however. Instead, back at his apartment, she invited Steve to have a conversation about what had happened. "I'd love to hear about what came up for you back there," she said to him. "Would you be willing to talk about it?"

Steve admitted that the image of Elizabeth in conversation with another man was pretty exciting to him. So was the idea of that man watching as the two of them hit it off and left the place together. He was embarrassed to admit, though, that part of him was worried she'd end up meeting somebody else she would rather go home with instead of him.

Elizabeth reassured Steve that going home with someone else was the furthest thing from her mind. She told him she'd still love to act out her fantasy with him "to show you just how into you I really am—and why you have nothing to worry about." She assured him that if they got to the bar and he still wasn't ready, she'd be totally okay with that. She was just happy he was willing to give it another try.

This isn't the only fantasy that the couple has now played out together. "I happen to have a lot of them," Elizabeth laughs. "As Steve says, we're having a hell of a good time!"

Elizabeth offers some insight into what can help someone say yes to an invitation. "What I've found is that Steve will go along with my little adventures as long as he knows that my real interest is in having an exciting experience with *him*."

Here are three more examples of how someone might express their desire through an invitation:

- Instead of "You never _____ anymore when we're making love like you used to," try "Remember how you used to _____ when we made love? I would absolutely love it if you did that again— like, right now!"

- Instead of "I've suggested this before and you weren't interested, but . . . ," try "I love imagining you in the role of _____. What could I do to entice you into acting that out with me sometime?"

- Instead of "I know you don't go for these kinds of things, but there's this tantra workshop for couples being held in the city next month," try "I love when we explore new things sexually. Do you want to go online with me to check out this couple's work-shop and see if it might be fun for us?"

Hailey, a dance instructor, has practiced using invitation often with Dakota, her partner of many years. "Sexy invitations have a special magic—they can be irresistible," she says. "And for us, fulfill-ing our fantasies together is just incredibly fun."

Of course, whether or not to ask your lover if they'd like to participate in fulfilling a particular desire will depend on what that desire is and the relationship you and your lover have. You'll have to decide whether your relationship—and your lover—seem as if they could be ready for what you have in mind.

INVITATION AND THE DESIRE TO BE SEEN

We all have a natural desire to be acknowledged and appreciated, to have our partner truly *see* us. We're not talking about the constant need for validation that can come from low self-esteem; we're talking about our natural, healthy desire for human connection. (Some people believe we should try to rise above our desire for others to see and acknowledge us. But for most of us mortals, that's just too lofty a goal, and may not sound like much fun.)

The reality is, it's not uncommon for couples to get into a routine and stop really noticing each other after a while. So if you ever feel as if your partner doesn't seem to be *seeing* you and instead is just seeing *through* you, here are some approaches you can try:

Start by taking in all the times they *do* acknowledge and appreciate you, even if only in small ways, and be grateful for them. You might be surprised how often people in relationships say, "I feel unappreciated for all the times I *do* notice him/her."

Additionally, don't assume that just because your partner doesn't seem to notice something about you (by, say, not complimenting you on it as they would have in the past) that means they no longer appreciate that aspect of you. What's more likely is that they have simply become used to it. Psychologists call this phenomenon *sensory adaptation*: our natural human tendency to become less responsive to the same stimulus over time.

What's important to recognize is this: when your partner does not seem to be noticing something he or she used to love about you, it's not necessarily a reflection of how they feel about you. And if it's something they appreciated in the past, they can probably appreciate it again. Understanding this can keep you from slipping into disappointment or resentment and instead give you the courage to invite them to see it again. If appreciation is not freely offered, if you have to go asking for it, you may feel

> If your partner doesn't seem to be seeing a certain aspect of you, *invite them to.*

it has less value. But it has far more value—for both you *and* your relationship—than resentment or disappointment ever will.

"It can be really hard to point out to my husband something I like about myself," admits Karen. "But if I don't, I end up feeling sad and disappointed. And when I do, he always seems happy to hear about it." And her husband? He says he appreciates the invitations. "When Karen tells me about something she did that she's proud of or shows me something she likes about herself, it makes me stop and look at her differently."

Here are a few examples of how a person might invite their partner to see something he or she might be overlooking:

- Instead of "You walked right by my new design without saying a word," try "Tell me when you have a few minutes. I really want to share my new design with you."

- Instead of "I got all dressed up for the party tonight and you didn't even notice," try "I feel almost like a different person in these new clothes—check this out!"

- Instead of "You never check out my butt anymore like you used to," try "I think you're really going to like how good my butt looks in these new jeans!"

With an invitation like one of these, with no attachment to whether or not your partner takes you up on it, you're not manipulating them into doing something they don't want to do. You're simply inviting them to take another look and maybe see something they didn't see before.

INVITING YOUR LOVER TO SEE ANOTHER POSSIBILITY

You probably know that trying to change someone, unless and until they ask for your help, is nearly impossible. Through your own example, however, you can sometimes invite someone to see another possibility.

Aidan, for example, believes that their sex life would improve if he and his boyfriend took better care of themselves; they both tire easily and often have little energy left for sex. But any time he's tried to suggest that the two of them should eat a healthier diet or get more exercise, it's just made John feel criticized and judged.

Finally, Aidan decided to simply make some changes on his own, and eventually

> Often the most loving and effective way to encourage your partner to make a positive change is through the power of your own example.

the results began to show: he started to look trimmer and stronger, and he had a lot more energy. A few weeks into the new routine, John asked what he was doing differently.

"He wanted in," laughs Aidan. "He didn't want to be left behind."

Whether it's an increase in exercise, a better diet, getting more rest, drinking less alcohol, or anything else you know would be good for your health, it often takes tremendous effort to make positive changes. As long as you don't push your new choices on him or her, your partner can—and very often will—draw inspiration and willpower from your own effort.

"It makes me stop and think when my girlfriend says no to a second glass of wine," says Cameron. "And when she gets up early on Saturday morning for her exercise class, it motivates me to drag my lazy butt out of bed and go work out too."

As Aidan and Cameron both know, sometimes our own example is all the invitation our partner needs.

———— ❦ ————

By harnessing the power of invitation, you will find
you have tremendous ability to create the relationships—and the life—
you truly desire.

10

The Art of Sexual Healing

Sexual healing isn't something you have to travel to the mountaintop to study. In fact, it's something that you and your lover can easily learn on the job! By using your sexual connection to heal each other, you'll be able to turn sexual "issues" into opportunities to deepen your intimacy and love.

"No one had ever brought me to orgasm before Paul showed up in my life."

Robin was in her early thirties when she met the man who's been her lover now for over a decade.

"I've never had trouble masturbating, but the idea of having a man bring me to orgasm seemed like a totally different thing," she recalls. "Whenever I'd see a movie or hear about it from my friends, I always wondered what the secret was. I'd talk about it and read about it and try to figure it out. But I never really thought of focusing on myself. In my mind, sex was all about the guy."

Then Robin met Paul, who was several years older than her and more mature than any of her previous lovers.

"He came along and said, 'Don't think about me; I'll be fine. Let's concentrate on you.' He got me to stop worrying about whether I was pleasing him and start getting in touch with what *I* liked, something I'd never even considered before."

It took almost a year with Paul, Robin says, before she had that first orgasm.

"First I had to learn to stop thinking and focus on the feeling. Then I had to let go of the particular 'routine' I'd always used and let an orgasm happen in a totally new way. Paul kept encouraging me to take all the time I needed to learn to let go of control, to trust enough to let *him* be the one to make it happen."

It's clear that Paul's patient, loving encouragement made all the difference.

"It was a big discovery for me to feel so much excitement and joy and comfort around my own sexuality," Robin says. "It's so much fun to finally be in the club."

SO JUST WHAT IS SEXUAL HEALING?

Although Robin and Paul might not have considered what they experienced together to be sexual healing, that's exactly what it was. Sexual healing can involve helping a lover with any issue related to sexuality, whether physical, psychological, or emotional.

In addition to helping each other experience more pleasure, as in

Robin's story, lovers can help heal misconceptions or limiting beliefs they have about themselves or their sexuality. They might explore a fear or break through a limitation together; uncover and transform feelings of low self-esteem, guilt, shame, envy, jealousy, or insecurity; or even discover ways to heal lingering issues from the past.

Sexual healing doesn't benefit just the person being healed. It also gives the healer love, gratitude, and a feeling of immense satisfaction. As Robin happily recalls, "It was so exciting for Paul to be the first man to ever make me come."

Healing doesn't have to mean fully resolving a particular issue. It often means just healing the *attitude* with which we approach it.

Tricia, who is large-breasted, has spent years trying to find bras and styles that help disguise her chest size. When she and her girlfriend recently went shopping for lingerie, they found themselves laughing hysterically as they attempted to stuff Tricia's ample "girls" into the shop's tight-fitting corsets.

"My boobs were spilling out everywhere," Tricia laughs. "What was so healing about that experience was being able to *celebrate* my size rather than trying to *minimize* it."

Sexual healing can involve something as simple as helping your lover explore a fear or inhibition.

"When Jim detects there's someplace where I'm holding myself back, he goes after it with great love and determination," says Annie about her husband of almost twenty years. "You know, I used to love dancing. But as I've gotten older, I've become more self-conscious. So he has me dress in something I still feel good in, put on music I love, and dance in front of him. With his help, I'm able to let go of my fear and reconnect with my love of dancing."

"She's just as beautiful to watch now as she ever was," Jim says. "And I have to tell you, it really puts us in the mood!"

Sexual healing can also involve learning to accept one's sexual fantasies or desires.

"When you have a specific 'kink' and are allowed to explore it without shame or fear, you expand your understanding of yourself," says Marie, a freelance journalist. "I've been aware of my own 'kink' all my life. As a child, I was shamed and shut down. As an adult, I was free to explore my interest. But without a partner who could 'go there' with me, or at least 'be there' with me, I couldn't really do it in a way that gave me a better understanding of myself.

> When you heal on a sexual level, you heal on spiritual, emotional, and physical levels as well.

"When I met my husband, I was finally able to just be me, because my kink doesn't scare or offend him. And even though it isn't something he would have chosen to explore on his own, he is happy to know me more intimately by exploring it with me."

Marie understands that bringing the darkest parts of ourselves into the light in the presence of our lover bonds us at a level of intimacy beyond what many couples ever experience.

"I'm so happy to be able to express myself with a committed partner," she says. "This has led me to physical, emotional, and spiritual heights I didn't know were possible."

As you can see, sexual healing often involves bringing our most intimate thoughts, feelings, and desires out into the open. For this to be possible, a safe, loving environment—one in which you both feel free to express yourselves authentically, to be vulnerable and open—is essential. Such an environment makes your relationship a source of continuous opportunities for healing and growth.*

SEXUAL HEALING AND SELF-ACCEPTANCE

Let's look at one of the most common areas where a little sexual healing could make a huge difference: our attitudes toward our own bodies.

Gina is a salon owner who's been doing bikini waxes for over two decades. "My clients' most common question, and one I hear every single day," she says, "is *Do I look normal?* I tell them that every woman looks different, and every woman is normal. Not only normal, but beautiful in her own way."

You can bet that after hearing this reassurance, Gina's clients leave feeling much better about themselves.

As Gina knows, there is tremendous variety in the shape, size, and color of women's sexual organs. It's even been said that vulvas are as unique as faces. So why do so many women think their vulvas are "abnormal," "ugly," or "weird looking"?

---

* *The Soulmate Experience: A Practical Guide to Creating Extraordinary Relationships* explores in depth how to create and maintain a safe, loving, supportive relationship space.

What we consider normal and desirable is largely a result of what we've been exposed to. But the majority of women see other women's genitals only in photos. And these days, most of those photos are digitally altered to make things look "neater," smaller, and more symmetrical. This means that women as well as men are getting a distorted picture of what's really "normal." In fact, the idealized image of what a vulva should look like has led to one of today's fastest-growing cosmetic surgeries: labiaplasty, the surgical trimming of the vaginal lips to produce a "cleaner" look.

If we believe that our body is inadequate or unacceptable in some way, we won't be able to open up to our full sexual potential with our lover.

Joshua, a commercial artist who also teaches life drawing at a small community college, says he doesn't like these trends—in either photography or surgery.

"What we're seeing is the homogenizing of vaginas," he explains. "Women's vulvas are individual works of art. Making them all look the same takes away their uniqueness. It's like making every wine taste the same. What's left to appreciate if everything unique has been 'tidied up'?"

Labiaplasty doesn't only remove a woman's "uniqueness." As the labia have a high concentration of nerve endings, this surgery can also result in a loss of sensation.

If you're a woman who has difficulty seeing her vulva as attractive, imagine how intimate and healing it could be to spend time with your lover exploring what makes your sexual organs uniquely beautiful. You might also check out the work of photographers whose images of real women's vulvas are intended to celebrate the natural beauty of this part of the body. When you see the incredible variety, you'll understand that you're not only normal, but beautiful as well.

Of course, it's not only women who can have trouble accepting a certain part of their body.

For example, a significant percentage of men with average-size penises actually believe that they're smaller than average. You might recall from Chapter 8 that pornography, which typically features actors with penises that are much larger than average, is responsible for a lot of this misperception. Add to that the general emphasis on penis size in our culture, and it would be difficult to grow up as an average-sized male and *not* feel self-conscious.

> In a loving, accepting environment, sexual intimacy presents the perfect opportunity for healing limiting beliefs about ourselves.

So if you're a guy who believes his equipment is smaller than average, do some research. If you find out you're actually average, you'll know that the "insufficiency" is really between your ears, not between your legs. And continuing to believe in that insufficiency is one of the worst things you can do for your sex life.

If you really are significantly smaller than average, and your worries about your size have kept you from enjoying a satisfying sex life, take heart. There are plenty of women (or men) who aren't focused on size and who will be interested in exploring all kinds of sexual pleasure with you. And who will be willing and even excited to be the one to help you let go of any limiting beliefs about yourself and your value that you may have developed over the years. (Especially after you've enticed them to read this chapter!)

It is in fact what we call our "issues" that give us a reason to practice sexual healing. *Healing on a sexual level is one of the most connecting and rewarding things you can do with a lover.* It brings two people together in a very intimate way.

"I know that size matters to some women, but it's just never been important to me," says Amanda, a doctor in her late thirties.

"Before I met Amanda, I always felt that my small size significantly limited what I could offer a woman sexually," admits Amanda's husband, Scott. "But she's taught me that sex is about so much more than just intercourse. When it comes to our sex life, we experiment a lot. We play. We have a great time together. Now I see that my insecurity about my size really kept me from being the best lover I could be."

One of the healing techniques Amanda came up with and uses from time to time is to have Scott lie back and fully surrender to the pleasure of oral sex. His only responsibility (and the only thing Amanda allows him to do) is to let go of any and all thoughts about his size and just enjoy the bliss of being made love to in such an erotic way.

The more self-confidence you help your partner to develop, the more attractive he or she will be to you.

170

As Amanda has learned, helping a lover heal limiting ideas they have about themselves or their body can have magical results:

"I'm more than happy to continue helping him to enjoy his body and our passionate sexual connection," says Amanda. "Because the more confident he gets, the more and more attractive he becomes to me."

So if your lover rejects their body in some way, don't pass up the chance to help them heal—or you'll miss a very special opportunity for connection.

SEXUAL HEALING 101

That all sounds great, you may be thinking, but how do I actually *do* sexual healing? Where do I even begin?

The first step is to get yourself into a sexual healing frame of mind. You do this by approaching whatever the issue is with love and acceptance, and as an opportunity to explore and connect with your lover. Keep in mind that it's often not the actual situation that you'll be healing; you can't instantly transform someone's body, for example, or erase a traumatic experience they've had. But you might very well be able to help them begin to heal their *attitude* toward themselves or that event.

If your lover is open to a little exploration, start out by helping him or her identify what their thoughts and beliefs around the issue are.

Suppose Craig, for example, knows that his girlfriend, Nicole, believes her breasts are too small. If she is willing to explore that belief with him, he could lovingly encourage her to identify exactly what she tells herself about her size. She might come up with thoughts like these: "I'd be more attractive if my breasts were bigger." "Women with smaller breasts aren't as sexy as women with larger ones." "You'd be more likely to stay in love with me if my breasts were larger."

Once your lover has uncovered the variety of thoughts they have around the issue, you might want to offer them some reassurance. Ask them to take in what you have to say without mentally or verbally rejecting it, to simply accept that this is what you believe. Craig, for example, might share with Nicole that he adores her as she is, and that he knows that many other people also think small breasts are beautiful.

Next, help your lover take a look at how their thoughts and beliefs make them feel. In our example, Craig could ask Nicole how she feels about herself when she thinks her breasts are too small, to which she might respond with something like "I feel inadequate, as if I'm not really a woman, or as if I'm not feminine enough."

Then explore what negative effects this limiting belief may have had on your lover's relationships. Nicole might recall times that her negative body image has caused her to feel embarrassed around other women, kept her from wearing certain clothes, or held her back from being fully comfortable naked. If strong or difficult emotions come up while you're working together, that's normal and perfectly okay. Just be there with your lover, hold them, and allow the emotions to be expressed and released; there's nothing you need to fix or solve.

Now help your lover imagine how they would feel if they "traded up" this idea about themselves for a better one—meaning one that would give them a better experience. Craig might ask, "How would your life be different if you believed your breasts were the perfect size?" If Nicole has trouble imagining this, Craig could reassure her that she doesn't have to believe this new idea; they're simply exploring how a different belief might make her feel. Eventually, Nicole might come up with something like "Well, I'd feel sexier and more comfortable in my body. And I'd probably love wearing bikinis, instead of avoiding them."

Through this process, you're demonstrating that what your lover believes about themselves is a choice, and that that choice has consequences. Just coming to this recognition can help someone begin to change their own beliefs around a particular issue and, as a result, feel much better about themselves.

Gratitude is another very effective sexual healing tool. To access its healing power, explore with your lover any positive aspects of the part of themselves they have an issue with. Craig and Nicole might talk about the advantages of having smaller breasts—like not suffering the backaches that some women have, or enduring discomfort from running or other exercise, or having the option of going braless when she wants to.

> Making love to a part of your lover's body that they have rejected can be profoundly healing.

Healing through sexual intimacy can be especially powerful. Whether it's your lover's breasts, face, or feet, make love to just that part while guiding them to let go of any

Use a Healing Affirmation   Repeating an affirmation to your lover can help shift you both into a sexual healing state of mind.

To guide your lover into relaxing and feeling safe, you might softly say,

- "There is nowhere else you need to be, nothing else you need to do."
- "Your only responsibility is to relax and enjoy all the sensations flowing through your body."

To help your lover let go of limiting ideas about his or her body, you might whisper,

- "You are here tonight to be cherished and loved."
- "I invite you to see all the beauty that I see in you."

negative thoughts that arise and to fully receive the love you're offering. What you're doing is creating an association between this part of their body and the experience of love, compassion, and pleasure.

You can also use a healing affirmation when you're making love. Craig might say these words to Nicole several times, slowly, allowing time for them to really sink in: "Nicole, your breasts are the perfect size to be loved."

Finally, try directing your love and sexual energy through your hands and into that part of your lover's body. The tremendously positive effects this can have might just surprise you both.

Sexual healing is a deeply personal and profound experience. Once you begin to experiment with it, you will find yourself creating your own healing techniques specifically suited to each situation. Here are some examples from people who have done this:

"Sometimes I'll make love to just her scars," says Tom, whose wife had a double mastectomy just after their second child was born. "It's such a sweet and emotional thing for us. She can feel my love and know that I find her just as sexy as I ever did."

Luis, who is married to a woman with breasts of noticeably different sizes, shares his own unique approach to sexual healing. "I pretend she's two different women," he says. "First I make love to the woman with smaller breasts, then to the woman with larger breasts. It's a definite turn-on for both of us."

And Tracy, whose husband was paralyzed in a car accident several years ago, says their sexual connection since the accident has been very healing for both of them. "This is the man I love," she says, "and just because he's paralyzed doesn't mean sex is over for us. I won't go into any detail, but I can say that I'm up for exploring all sorts of things with him and that we have a very satisfying sex life. It's a really special and sacred thing between us."

SEXUAL HEALING AND ERECTION ISSUES

Before meeting Ellen, Ron had always been a premature ejaculator, typically climaxing within twenty or thirty seconds of being inside a woman. Ellen and Ron had made love a few times before Ellen asked him about it. He confessed that it wasn't only his excitement about being with her that was causing his quick finishes. This was, unfortunately, just normal for him.

Instead of being discouraged by this news, Ellen got curious. Just what might help him last a little longer?

"He didn't believe in his ability to hold off, but I did," she says mischievously. "So I enticed him to try things that would break the cycle. I made him kiss every part of my body as long as I wanted him to before he was allowed to enter me. Or I'd stroke and kiss every part of his body, but only as long as he was describing to me exactly what I was doing to him. If he stopped talking, I stopped touching."

What Ellen was doing was giving the sexual energy between the two of them time to build. She was also helping Ron to be more aware of that energy in his body so that he could learn to develop control.

Ellen describes a time she and Ron made love while he was on his back and she was on top. "We were there for hours," she recalls. "I would rock back and forth only as long as he kept his excitement under control. The moment he started to really respond, I'd stop until he relaxed and his breathing slowed down again. It was so much fun, a sensual, erotic tease. And it worked."

For Ron, realizing that he actually *could* have intercourse for longer than a minute or two—in fact, over a period of several hours—allowed him to "become conscious of easing off before the point of no return."

From his healing experiences with Ellen, he's learned that "I have much more control than I ever thought I had."

In the years since, whenever they've drifted back into the habit of too many "quickies" in a row, Ellen has enjoyed "slowing him down all over again."

Of course, premature ejaculation can have many underlying causes, from psychological issues like stress or performance anxiety to medical conditions like diabetes. But with a healing attitude and an environment of kindness, love, and fun, lovers can approach the sexual aspects of any of these situations not as a problem but as an exploration.

Here is another example of sexual healing around an issue that many men have faced from time to time:

A couple of years into Kelly and Daniel's relationship, Daniel started having more and more difficulty maintaining an erection. Kelly says that when she first tried to talk to him about it, "there seemed to be quite a sense of shame around the issue for him. He actually did see a doctor, but to him the idea of having to use a drug to get an erection would mean he was a failure as a man."

One day, though, when they were excitedly planning an upcoming vacation, Kelly suggested they bring along a couple of little blue pills, just as something fun to experiment with.

To his surprise, Daniel found that taking the medication helped him to relax and stop worrying about whether he'd be able to perform. These days, he says, "just knowing it's available makes me more confident, so I find I rarely need it."

Obviously, this solution won't work for everyone. Difficulty in achieving or maintaining an erection can be caused by high blood pressure, low testosterone, stress, or other factors that might require professional help. But no matter what the cause, a lover's no-fault, let's-have-fun-with-this attitude can be very healing.

HEALING FROM THE PAST

Peter and Susan met in the bookstore where they both work part time. Peter, who is sixty-two, is also an artist and a gardener. He's a gentle, soft-spoken man who has never been married and is very content with his quiet life. Susan is thirty-eight. At nineteen, she had finally gotten enough courage to leave home and her sexually abusive father. Since then, she's had two significant relationships, both with men who eventually began to verbally and physically abuse her.

When Susan and Peter met, they had both been single for several years: Susan because she'd decided that men just weren't safe, and Peter because he hadn't met anyone he felt passionate about in a long time.

Their friendship began with enjoying tea together in the bookstore during their breaks. They started going out to dinner once in a while and found they really enjoyed each other's company.

After hearing a little about Susan's past, Peter instinctively knew that, more than anything else, "she needed to experience feeling completely safe around a man." As they continued to spend time together, their feelings for each other grew. They would hold hands and cuddle, sometimes for hours. Although he found himself quite attracted to Susan, Peter remained committed to keeping their relationship nonsexual.

Sexual healing can be as simple as creating a space for your partner to have a new experience.

"Just being held by a man with love and kindness was obviously very healing for her," he explains. "She'd never experienced that before in her life."

With Peter, Susan felt she could let her guard down and allow herself to completely relax, knowing that nothing bad was going to happen.

Susan learned something immensely valuable through her friendship with Peter. "Being with him introduced me to an entirely new kind of relationship, one based on mutual love and respect," she says. "Now I know that I'm capable of recognizing a nice man when I meet one."

Peter says this experience was just as healing for him. Being his age, he explains, "the fires of passion don't burn as brightly as they used to. I was happy to discover that it is still possible for me to feel that depth of desire for someone."

The time he spent with Susan, Peter says, "opened me to the possibility of having a different sort of intimate relationship than I'd had in the past. Before, if the passion wasn't there immediately, I just assumed it wasn't worth pursuing. Now I realize that, at this stage of my life, it may just take a little more time for the passion to really ignite."

Although Susan and Peter's story is unusual, in it we can see an essential element of sexual healing: *A safe, loving, accepting space, in which you both can be authentic and vulnerable, creates a perfect opportunity for deep and lasting healing.*

AGING: RESISTANCE IS FUTILE, SO ATTITUDE IS EVERYTHING

It can be easy to slip into the mindset that getting old just plain sucks. How we choose to respond to aging won't change the inevitability of it, but it will immensely affect our experience of it. The following easy attitude adjustments can give you the very best experience possible:

- *Approach aging as an adventure.* You've probably met couples in their seventies who seem as though they're in their fifties because they're so passionate about life. They are living proof that the life inside you has nothing to do with the age of your skin or the gray in your hair. Since it's coming anyway, why not go into menopause—or for men, andropause—with a sense of curiosity instead of fear? With a change of perspective, you might be able to *appreciate* a hot flash as an intensely physical sensory experience. Or you might look forward to seeing how you and your lover evolve over the years. And the next time you find yourself examining your newest wrinkles in the mirror, using your age as an excuse not to try something new, or negatively comparing yourself to someone years younger, see if you can look at the changes you're going through as just another part of the adventure.

- *See the beauty in people older than you.* If you believe that youth is what makes someone attractive, you won't feel attractive when you're older. So practice seeing men and

> Premature aging starts in your mind.

180

women older than you as attractive. Start noticing the beauty in them, and it will be much easier to see yourself and your lover as attractive as you age together.

- *Actively appreciate and inspire each other.* How do you stay attracted to someone you've seen so much of? If you want your partner to continue to *be* sexy, you've got to continue to *see* them as sexy. And help them see it in themselves. "When I confess I'm thinking I'm not as attractive as when I was younger," says Jamie, "Alex will say something like, 'The beauty that radiates from within you is timeless' or 'Your body has brought me more pleasure over the years than I can possibly remember' or 'I can't think of anybody else I'd rather get old with.' Hearing that makes me feel a whole lot better." Laura, who raised three children with her husband, Dean, says they practice seeing each other as spiritual beings in bodies that are going through the normal aging process. "When I look at Dean and

> Worrying about the youth you don't have is a waste of the youth you do have.

Move It to Your Love Wardrobe Don't toss that flirtatious skirt or the dress with the low-cut neckline just because society has you believing they're too revealing for someone your age. Instead, move them from your regular wardrobe to your "love wardrobe." And don't wait for a special occasion to change into your sexy stuff—*make* it a special occasion by slipping into that sheer, lacy thing for a romantic dinner at home.

feel that spiritual part of him," says Laura, "it's as though he hasn't aged at all, no matter how much his body has changed."

- *Keep your sexual connection alive.* As long as they have been together, Lisette and Richard have had a desire to stay sexually connected as they age—for themselves as much as for each other. "We've been together almost twenty-seven years, and we have a vision of enjoying our sex life for as long as we can," says Lisette. "We make time to nurture that aspect of our life together. It doesn't mean you have to try weird things or things you aren't comfortable with, but you can have great sex at any age. I truly believe sex is better for us now than it has ever been." Lisette and Richard aren't alone. There are plenty of older couples who report that they're having the best sex of their lives.

- *See your faces as evolving works of art.* Look at your lover's face—the familiar features, the lines, the things that have changed since you first met—as you would look at a sculpture or a painting. You might

---

Make Love Through the Decades Couples who meet later in life sometimes express regret at not having known each other earlier. If you can relate to this, or if you've been with your lover a long time, spend an evening bringing the past alive. Surround yourself with photos of your partner at different ages. Explore them together, trying to get a feeling for who this person was at each age. Then make love to all of them in turn—the carefree 22-year-old college boy, the independent 32-year-old bachelor, the handsome 42-year-old father—and connect with each of them as an aspect of the person you love.

---

try putting into words how the things you love about this person are reflected in their face: "When I look at you, I see all the experiences we've had together." Or "I get this sense of all the things you've loved in your life." Do the same for yourself, looking in the mirror and knowing that all your life experiences—the everyday ones, the challenging ones, the amazing ones—had a hand in shaping this unique work of art.

> **Keep seeing all the beauty in your beloved and you'll be in love with someone truly beautiful.**

One last piece of inspiration comes from Suzanne, a mother of two who came to parenthood later in life. "I was at a pool party recently, and I was the only mom to wear a swimsuit or get in the pool," she says. "I remember being in my twenties and thirties and not wearing a swimsuit. It must have had something to do with feeling I didn't look good enough. At almost fifty, I finally feel I've 'earned' the right to wear the smallest of bikinis. My comfort in my body these days has everything to do with a head full of thoughts like 'Wow, this amazing body has given me this beautiful family!'"

SEXUAL HEALING
IS A CONTINUAL EXPLORATION

Sexual healing isn't just a one-time thing: it's an ongoing opportunity to create deeper connection. Robin, whose lover Paul helped her learn how to relax and tune in to her body so she could have an orgasm with him rather than just on her own, understands this.

"After about a year, I could come through oral sex, but it wasn't consistent," she explains. "I couldn't always get there; sometimes I was still too distracted by my thoughts."

Fortunately for Robin, Paul was devoted to the cause. "We kept practicing," Robin says, "until I finally learned how to let go and focus entirely on the feeling."

Even though orgasms through oral sex now happen regularly, Robin and Paul's explorations into sexual healing aren't over. "Although I've been able to have a vaginal orgasm with the help of a vibrator," she explains, "I've still never had one through intercourse. It might be physiology that keeps me from getting there, but even if I never do, it's very connecting to keep exploring it together. It's still fun to try!"

When you get a feel for sexual healing, you will realize that it's about more than helping each other heal certain attitudes or issues. It's also about the intimacy, love, and gratitude you will both experience through the process.

11

Opening Up to
Your Orgasmic Potential

*Wherever you are along the orgasm spectrum—whether you
struggle to have them at all or feel very satisfied with your
experiences so far—there are many things you can do, both on
your own and with a lover, to expand your orgasmic potential and
experience more frequent, more intense, and more profound orgasms.*

"I always thought I was just a freak."

Melissa, a magazine editor, belongs to the relatively small percentage of women who say they are multiorgasmic.

"I remember having my first orgasm—which was also the first time I ever had intercourse—and thinking, 'Oh my God, so *that's* why people make such a big deal about sex!'"

It wasn't long, though, before Melissa began to worry there might be something not quite "normal" about her.

"Sure, I knew about orgasm, but I'd never heard it described the way *I* was experiencing it. As soon as I'd start to have intercourse,

I'd start to come. I had so much shame around the idea of being this weird freak of nature. I remember my old boyfriend telling my new boyfriend, 'It doesn't really count when Melissa has an orgasm. She just has them.'"

You might think Melissa has nothing to complain about, but from her perspective, she missed out on a lot. She was almost fifty before she realized she hadn't taken full advantage of all the pleasure her body was capable of feeling. Every one of her intimate relationships, she believes, would have been more sexually fulfilling had she had, in her words, a "proper orgasm education."

"I would have understood that every woman is unique and that I was perfectly okay the way I was. I would have enjoyed exploring my sexuality instead of always holding myself back. I would have made sexual compatibility a priority in choosing a life partner. And I certainly wouldn't have ended up marrying a man who didn't even like sex."

Melissa felt uncomfortable around her sexuality because she orgasmed so easily. Though she may be in the minority in that regard, Melissa has something in common with other women who experience anxiety because of their difficulties with orgasm. They all suffer from embarrassment, disappointment, or shame about how their bodies respond sexually.

Whether you're naturally orgasmic or not, becoming more comfortable with your body's unique sexual response is one important aspect of opening up to your full orgasmic potential: your capacity to experience more frequent, more intense, and more profound orgasms.

WE COULD ALL USE A LITTLE MORE "ORGASM EDUCATION"

Orgasm is a fascinating and even somewhat mysterious topic, surrounded by all sorts of speculation (along with some disagreement), even among sex educators and researchers.

The word *orgasm* refers to the release of built-up sexual tension through the contraction of muscles in the pelvic area. During an orgasm, which typically lasts several seconds for men and on average around twenty seconds for women, men experience three to six orgasmic contractions and women from four to twenty. In both men and women, orgasms trigger the release of hormones that give them a sense of well-being and leave them feeling relaxed and content.

People's experiences with orgasm can vary tremendously. For instance, around 15 to 25 percent of women report having multiple orgasms, while 5 to 10 percent say they have never climaxed at all. And estimates vary, but around 75 percent of women don't reach orgasm through intercourse without some type of stimulation of the clitoris, such as through the touch of their own or their lover's hand.

Besides the fact that some people reach orgasm more easily than others, people also describe their orgasms in vastly different ways. Their experiences differ not only from person to person, but from orgasm to orgasm. For example, Tami, who is in her thirties, says, "Mine are always most intense right before my period."

Though men's experiences may not vary as much as women's, there are factors that can affect the quality of their orgasms too.

Anthony reports, "For me it's pretty simple. More foreplay gives me stronger, longer-lasting erections and more powerful orgasms."

"When I'm able to get out of my head and into a rhythm," says James, "and especially if we're feeling really connected, my orgasms stretch out and are way more intense. It feels like they completely take me over."

Some women describe two types of orgasm, clitoral and vaginal. Others say their orgasm experiences can't be classified into specific types. "My 'shower spray' orgasm is in a class all by itself," laughs Janine.

Women who report having vaginal orgasms often mention the G-spot. This area is found an inch or two inside the vagina, along the front wall. When stimulated through intercourse, the use of a vibrator, or the stroking of a lover's finger, the G-spot can produce pleasurable sensations in some women and orgasms in others. There are experts who aren't convinced this area even exists, but all that really matters is whether this spot—or any other highly erogenous area—is pleasurable for *you*.

> Sexual exploration is about discovering your own pleasure spots, which can be different every time you make love.

A similarly sensitive area in men is the prostate gland. Often called the male G-spot, this region can provide intense pleasure and contribute to more powerful orgasms when stimulated, either from inside (such as with a finger or a sex toy designed for this purpose) or by massaging the perineum (the area just behind the testicles).

For men, of course, the peak of orgasm is usually accompanied by ejaculation. We say "usually" because some men do, on occasion, orgasm without ejaculating (what's called a dry orgasm).

And what about women? Though not all experts agree that female ejaculation even occurs, there are countless women who report that it does. Where the fluid is produced and what it consists of is still being studied and debated, but for women who have experienced this, it can be helpful to know that it is perfectly normal. (*Not* experiencing this is also perfectly normal.)

"The first time I ejaculated was a real surprise," recalls Melissa. "I didn't have a clue what was going on, and neither did my boyfriend. And there was no Internet to ask."

Then there are women, as well as some men, who can orgasm without any direct contact with their genitals.

"It's all about how turned on I am," says Lauren. "I've come just by having my nipples played with or my neck stroked, or even through a really great kiss. I've even had one in a restaurant when my husband was whispering in my ear what he was going to do to me when we got home!"

> The better your orgasm education, the more fun, passion, and pleasure you'll experience with a lover.

In studies using an MRI scanner, scientists have confirmed that there are also women who can have orgasms induced solely by their own thoughts and mental imagery. Some men say they are able to do this as well. In fact, most men have experienced ejaculation without being physically stimulated—during a nocturnal emission, or "wet dream."

There are also women who have had unintentional orgasms while exercising or doing yoga (giving us the expression "yogasms"). When Catherine heard about this from a friend, she was relieved. "I thought I was the only one!" she says.

If you struggle to achieve orgasm, or have never had one (yet), don't be discouraged by these stories. Instead, consider the possibility that there might be more paths to your own pleasure than perhaps you realized.

GETTING INTO THE "O" ZONE

Whether you're single or in a relationship, naturally orgasmic or orgasmically challenged, there are a number of steps you can take to increase your orgasmic potential. If you have a partner, exploring these ideas together can be incredibly intimate and connecting. If you're single, exploring by yourself has its own rewards. One of those rewards is that as you become more in touch with your own sexuality, attracting a truly compatible lover becomes much easier.

Step 1: Know Your Anatomy—Inside and Out

We can learn something about becoming more orgasmic by taking a look at what women who orgasm more easily tend to have in common. These ideas aren't only for women; they're just as valuable for men.

For one, women who orgasm easily are often more familiar with their own anatomy, especially the parts that are capable of bringing them intense pleasure. If you could use a refresher on your anatomy, do a search for some illustrations or labeled photographs. Then thoroughly check things out, using a mirror if it's helpful.

Let's start with the women. Choose a time when you're feeling relaxed and comfortable, and when it's unlikely you will be interrupted. Get yourself in the mood by lighting a couple of candles, putting on some music, or pouring yourself a glass of wine or a cup of tea.

If you can approach this exercise with a "beginner's mind," you might very well make some new discoveries about yourself. Begin your exploration with your vulva, which includes the labia majora and minora (outer and inner lips). The color, size, and shape of the labia vary tremendously from woman to woman. The vulva also changes over time and can look quite different at age forty than at age twenty. If you find it challenging to see yours as attractive, revisit "Sexual Healing and Self-Acceptance" in Chapter 10 for a reminder that every vulva is uniquely beautiful.

Explore different kinds of sensations. Stroke or pat your vulva with your palm. Roll the lips back and forth between your fingers; rhythmically squeeze and release them. You might apply some soft pressure with a warm, wet towel and enjoy the sweet feeling of relaxing into that supportive warmth, allowing that feeling to spread throughout your body. In the bath or shower, you'll discover that slowly pouring warm water over your vulva can feel heavenly.

As the only part of the human body (male or female) designed purely for pleasure, the clitoris is an amazing little piece of engineering. Make sure you're very familiar with yours (or your partner's). In addition to the parts you can see, the clitoris also includes touch receptors that extend

There's so much more to the clitoris than meets the eye!

beneath the surface in all directions, greatly expanding its range of sensitivity. Experiment with different kinds of touch and varying amounts of pressure all around the area (especially if, like most people, you're in the habit of doing things in a certain way). You might tease yourself with a feather, caress yourself with a silk scarf or other soft material, apply pressure with a smooth object, or massage in some natural oil. Be curious. Be playful. What feels good? What feels *really* good?

Some women describe different areas of their vaginas as having different types or degrees of sensitivity. Whether or not you've already discovered any particularly sensitive areas in yours, it's always worth checking back in, as things can change. To feel specifically for the G-spot, curve a finger (or your partner's finger) up toward your stomach and stroke the front wall of your vagina.

In addition to exploring with your fingers, you may want to do a little research and experiment with some of the many lubricants, vibrators, and other sex toys available for pleasuring your clitoris, vulva, and vagina. A massager that straps to the back of your hand is particularly nice to have around because it offers more sensitivity and control, while still having the intimacy of human touch.

Like a woman's body, a man's body has its own especially responsive areas. If you're a man, you might begin this exploration by pressing a warm towel against your genitals and relaxing into the exquisite feeling. Then, instead of focusing on getting an erection, try touching and exploring yourself as though it's the very first time.

Massaging, squeezing, and stroking, experiment with all the different sensations you can create, taking note of any places that are especially sensitive. Apply some oil or lotion and notice how that changes the sensations. Pinch, press, or massage your fingers into the firm area behind your testicles, through which you can indirectly stimulate your prostate gland (you may have to be somewhat aroused before you begin to feel anything). You might also take a look into the many different kinds of massagers and other sex toys that are specifically designed to enhance men's sexual pleasure.

The more intimate you become with your own body, the more enjoyable sex will be.

Sometimes exploring your anatomy is easier (and more fun) with a partner. Jay and Lily, for example, who have been married long enough to have raised two children together, have recently experimented with the male G-spot. Jay admits to being reluctant at first.

"I never would have thought I'd try something like this," he says. "But Lily read about it in a magazine, and we'd been talking about being more adventurous, so I kind of had to say yes."

And what does he think now? "I have to say, once I got over my initial hesitation, and Lily was able to get me to relax, my orgasm was explosive."

Step 2: Open Yourself to Receiving Pleasure—You're Worth It

Women who orgasm more easily also tend to be more at ease receiving their lover's attention. But Annette speaks for many women when she says, "I just can't relax when all his attention is on me, because my overriding thought is 'He can't really be enjoying this, can he?' He seems perfectly happy, but I still have this little feeling of guilt."

The truth is, he most certainly *can* be enjoying it. You might even want to ask him. You'll probably hear something like "Hell yes, I'm enjoying myself!" And on the off chance he says he isn't? If you want a healthy sexual relationship, you really are better off knowing. In fact, this could be a good opportunity for a heart-to-heart conversation about your sex life and how, together, you might bring more excitement and pleasure into it.

It's not just women who can be uncomfortable relaxing and allowing themselves to receive pleasure. "I always have this underlying idea

---

Squeeze Your Way to a Stronger Orgasm   You may know that women can strengthen their vaginal and other pelvic muscles by rhythmically squeezing them, an exercise called Kegels. But did you know that this same exercise can also lead to better ejaculation control in men? And to longer, stronger orgasms in both men and women? Doing Kegels regularly (and for women, trying a vaginal exerciser, such as small balls or weights designed to strengthen these muscles) also gives you more awareness and control in that area of your body—the kind of control that, with a little imagination, can surprise and excite your partner!

---

that we have to keep the amount of pleasure we each get in balance," says Thomas, a personal fitness trainer. "So if my girlfriend is doing something for me for longer than a few minutes, I start to feel like I'm getting more than I deserve and it's time to reciprocate."

> Sex is much more enjoyable, for you and your lover, when you believe you're worthy of receiving pleasure.

If you notice yourself worrying about reciprocating, remember that there will be plenty of time to make your partner the center of attention, and just let yourself surrender. You will enjoy it more, which means *they* will enjoy it more too.

If it feels right, you might also consider sharing with your lover any fears or feelings of shame or guilt that might be keeping you from fully relaxing and receiving their attention. In a safe and supportive environment, exploring your fears together can be one of the most intimate and bonding experiences two people can have (see Chapter 4, "Letting Go of Sexual Shame," and Chapter 10, "The Art of Sexual Healing").

Another suggestion comes from Zena, who tried hypnotherapy treatments for anorgasmia, or difficulty reaching orgasm.

"It's not that I couldn't have them at all," she says, "but so often I just couldn't quite get there. Hypnosis used the power of suggestion to help me feel a little more, to relax a little bit deeper, to let everything else go. It helped me learn to just let my body open up and allow the pleasure to happen."

Step 3: Be Willing to Ask for What You Want

Another similarity among women who have more frequent orgasms is that they understand that when you're willing to *ask* for what you want, you're much more likely to *get* what you want. If you're not used to verbalizing your desires, that knowledge should give you enough motivation to try it once in a while. You might just discover that your lover not only wants to know what you want, but is more than happy to provide it.

"We men are kind of fumbling around on our own a lot of the time," admits Andrew, a civil engineer. "A lot of us would be grateful for some honest guidance."

"It's always exciting when Christopher tells me exactly what he wants me to do to him," says Marlena, a pediatrician. "And even more exciting to give it to him!"

Program Yourselves for Pleasure   Practice being open to asking for and receiving what you want by taking turns being each other's "personal pleasure provider" for an hour or even an entire evening.

As the provider, your sole purpose is to bring your lover as much pleasure as possible, so invite him or her to guide you in any way.

As the receiver, this is your opportunity to get more comfortable expressing yourself, whether that's through the expressions on your face, the movements of your body, the sounds you make, or simply asking for what you want. It's also the time to practice receiving, so indulge yourself: take a risk, be vulnerable, and ask for your heart's—and your body's!—desire.

What might it look like to ask for what you want?

It might be that you request a little less pressure here or a little more pressure there. Or that you seductively whisper, in explicit detail, what would feel really good. Or that you take your lover's hands and guide them.

Asking for what you want might mean enticing your lover with an invitation: "I love the way you're kissing my shoulder right now. It would be so sexy if you moved that talented mouth of yours up to my neck" or "You know that thing you were doing a few minutes ago? Could you go back to that so I can properly express just how incredibly good that feels?"

Asking for what you want could also mean letting yourself scream, "YES YES YES!" if that's what you're inspired to do. Not only will this let your lover know how much you're enjoying yourself; he or she might also find it incredibly sexy. "It's really erotic to be doing something that's causing her to make sounds only a really turned-on woman would make," says Ralph, a fashion photographer.

If you're worried about waking the neighbors, screaming into a pillow is far better for your pleasure than holding yourself back!

Another way of expressing what you want is through your natural body language. Of course, it helps if your lover is in tune with you and able to interpret your nonverbal cues. If he or she isn't, why not offer a little loving guidance? For instance, "If you feel my body pressing toward you, keep on doing what you're doing!" Teaching your lover how to read your body language will not only make your encounters more pleasurable for you, it will also reward you with a more attentive lover.

Here's another reason to get comfortable communicating your desires: expecting your lover to know what you like or want can easily lead to frustration and disappointment. And we all know how well frustration and disappointment go over in the bedroom. Over time, such expectations can also lead to the buildup of resentment. So even if it's something you've mentioned many times before, don't get irritated and begin to shut down. You'll get much better results by learning to ask every time as if it's the very *first* time.

Step 4: Think Less, Feel More

Whether it's worries about our bodies, anxiety about our performance, or expectations about what will happen next, studies suggest that what's going on in our heads can be the cause of much of our difficulty with orgasm. As Jess says, "I've found that if my head is elsewhere, it's just not going to happen." The reason for this is simple: being preoccupied with what we're thinking takes us away from what we're experiencing. When you realize you're being distracted mentally, you might want to revisit the ideas and suggestions in "Move Out of Your Head to Get Present in Bed" in Chapter 8.

Alexis confesses that in her previous relationships, fear about how she might look when she was having an orgasm often kept her from fully letting go. "I just couldn't allow myself to get out of control and risk making a really strange face," she says.

When she started seeing John, however, she could tell that holding herself back from expressing her passion was keeping them from being as sexually connected as they could be. So she took a chance and confessed her fear to him.

"He assured me that seeing unbridled passion on a woman's face is the sexiest thing on earth," Alexis says. "If she lets herself express what she's feeling, he says, she's beautiful." Her boyfriend's reassurance helps Alexis to let go of any worries that might come up about what she looks like. "And when I'm not worried about what I look like," she reports, "we both have a lot more fun."

> You simply can't reach your full orgasmic potential when you're worried about how you look.
>
> ༄

By letting go of the thoughts in your head and focusing all your attention on what you're experiencing, you might discover that you've been feeling things you weren't fully aware of.

"When I started having sex, I didn't know that what I was experiencing *was* an orgasm; it wasn't the earth-shattering thing I'd been expecting," says Teresa, who is now in her thirties. "It actually took me a couple of years before I realized what was going on. Then I started paying more attention to those feelings, and over time they grew much stronger."

Teresa is not the only woman who has used the power of awareness to increase her own pleasure. If you've never or rarely experienced an orgasm, you might discover that the practice of thinking less and feeling more may one day make it possible for you to feel your way all the way to an orgasm.

Step 5: Make Orgasm an Exploration, Not a Destination

We often approach sex as a predictable progression: from first base to second base, from foreplay to intercourse, with orgasm as the ultimate goal (and the signal that the sexual encounter is over). This is not all that surprising, given that pretty much our entire culture supports this idea. But this "step by step" approach can quickly drain the spontaneity, mystery, and sense of adventure from any sexual relationship.

So rather than thinking of foreplay as something that *leads* to sex, think of foreplay simply *as* sex. In fact, try inviting your lover into bed for a little "sexplay." You'll probably find that something as simple as calling it "sexplay" instead of "foreplay" can actually inspire more passion and excitement.

Doesn't sexplay just sound like more fun than foreplay?

Making orgasm an exploration rather than a destination also means focusing a little less on the orgasm at the end and a little more on all the pleasure to be had along the way. It may seem ironic, but by putting less attention on orgasm and more on everything leading up to it, you're going to have stronger, more intense climaxes. And if orgasm is a challenge for you, focusing on just enjoying yourself and whatever pleasure you *are* experiencing will not only make your sexual experiences more fulfilling, it will also make reaching orgasm far more likely.

CULTIVATING SEXUAL ENERGY

In the ancient Chinese philosophy of Taoism, sexual energy is considered a powerful form of chi, or life energy. Expending too much of this energy too often will leave a person depleted, while developing an awareness of and an ability to conserve and cultivate sexual energy will increase a person's vitality and encourage deeper states of connection with a lover.

As we explore in "Cultivate Sexual Energy by Playing at the Edge of Orgasm" in Chapter 6, individuals can use masturbation to cultivate their sexual energy. Couples can also practice building and sustaining their sexual energy together to prolong their sexual experiences, heighten their pleasure, and deepen their intimacy. Modern-day tantra also emphasizes cultivating sexual energy, with a focus on couples using the practice to create a feeling of deep intimacy and even spiritual connection (which is why the practice is also sometimes called *sacred sexuality* or *spiritual sex*).

You and your lover could take a workshop on or read about various breathing, meditation, and visualization techniques for cultivating sexual energy and enhancing sexual pleasure. Or just explore and experiment to create your own techniques. Here are a few ideas to get you started: Hold each other and just breathe

Focusing your awareness on the energy flowing between you and your lover is a kind of sexual meditation.

together, following your breath as it moves in and out of your bodies, feeling your bodies move with your breathing. While looking into each other's eyes, kiss with your lips just barely touching. Caress, embrace, wrap yourselves around each other, allowing the love, desire, and sexual energy to flow freely between you.

Helping each other delay orgasm can be another deliciously sensual and connecting experience. Take each other just to the edge, then back off a little, then slowly start up again. As you practice this, you'll get to know each other's responses and be able to sustain the state of sexual arousal even longer.

Also experiment with different positions for intercourse, using pillows to support your bodies and help you both to relax. Try moving very slowly in each position, playing with different rhythms, or contracting and releasing your pelvic muscles. Enhance your experience by massaging each other while you're making love, breathing in unison, giving yourselves permission to make noise, moving to the rhythms of different kinds of music, or eye gazing (see "Connect Through Your Eyes" in Chapter 12).

In all of these practices, be aware of the feeling of sexual energy circulating throughout your bodies. A common tantric practice is to visualize your energy flowing from the pelvis up the spine and back down the front of the body. When you do release into orgasm, allow the sexual energy to radiate through your entire body. You might also visualize it spreading out and encompassing your partner as an expression of your love and gratitude for creating this experience with you.

> Cultivating sexual energy together will help you and your lover feel more connected, both sexually and spiritually.

RIDING THE WAVE OF ORGASM

Carla, who owns an import business, is in her early forties. She regularly experiences orgasms that "feel like they could go on indefinitely."

"It didn't used to be that way," she says. "In fact, for the first few years I was sexually active, I never had an orgasm at all."

What is Carla's secret?

"The best way I can put it is that it's something I've learned to 'allow,'" she explains. "There's a way in which I let go inside—of thought, or tension, or any ways I'm holding myself back. It's a process of surrendering. I have to just allow the orgasm to happen."

When we relax into an orgasm and let it move through us without restriction, taking us over, the experience can feel as if it goes beyond just the physical, into what some people call the ecstatic.

"Surrendering to orgasm is the difference between feeling it just in your genitals and feeling it through your entire body," says Noah, a lawyer in his thirties who's attended several seminars on sexuality. "Instead of it happening *to* you, it feels like it's happening *through* you. It's as if you *become* the orgasm."

It's not uncommon for men and women alike to tense up or "contract" when having an orgasm. Helping each other to relax into the experience instead, to fully open up to it, is a deeply satisfying practice.

To guide your partner to fully surrender into their orgasm, you might say something

> Encourage your lover to ride the wave of orgasm by creating a safe space for them to fully open up and let go.

203

like "Relax your face, let your breathing be natural and full. Let yourself sigh or moan. Feel the sensations wash over and through you; just surrender to them. This is a safe place for you to completely relax and let go."

Guiding one another to ride the wave of orgasm can be one of the most erotic and deeply passionate experiences you will

When you know how to charge your relationship with sexual energy, passion and desire become renewable resources!

ever create together. Yet it doesn't have to end there. Cuddling and caressing after sex, when all your senses are heightened and you're feeling close and connected, can be incredibly sensual and loving.

"We often enjoy touching until one of us falls asleep," says Sebastian. "It is a beautiful experience to witness your lover drift off to sleep in your arms."

If you're single, opening up to your orgasmic potential will help you attract a lover who is ready for a deeply connected sexual relationship. And knowing how to keep that relationship charged with sexual energy will continually renew your passion and desire for each other.

12

The Five Essential Practices for Truly Soulful Sex

*The five practices presented in this chapter are the foundation for
every idea in this book. They are also at the very heart of creating
and sustaining a passionate, loving, and deeply intimate relationship.*

Whether you've just started seeing someone new or have been
with your partner for many years, the five practices that follow will enhance every aspect of your relationship. The more you
weave these practices into your life, the more connected and alive
all your experiences together will be.

PRACTICE 1: ACCEPT WHAT IS

Wherever you are, whatever you're doing, you have the choice to
accept "what is" or to resist it.

Accepting "what is" doesn't mean you necessarily agree with or
condone a particular situation or give up your ability to improve it.

In fact, when you aren't spending your energy on resistance, you'll be in a much better position to assess the situation and decide if and how to respond. Any action you do decide to take will be guided by wisdom instead of being driven by emotions like frustration, jealousy, or anger.

Why is cultivating an attitude of acceptance so valuable in a sexual relationship? Because an environment of acceptance—an environment in which you both feel free to express yourselves authentically and to be vulnerable and open—is what makes true intimacy possible.

Being receptive and open-minded toward another person doesn't mean you necessarily agree with their opinions or approve of their actions. *Accepting another person simply means you recognize and acknowledge that this is who they are at this moment.*

Accepting another person also doesn't mean being naive or unrealistic. On the contrary, the practice of acceptance will help you to recognize when being intimate with someone *isn't* in your best interest. Instead of closing your eyes to unhealthy behaviors or attitudes, you see them and acknowledge them. This enables you to make wiser decisions about the relationship and even alter your involvement if you feel that's the best choice.

"It was hard to admit to myself that my wife, who had been having affairs for years, was unlikely to ever change," says Rick. "But finally accepting that freed me to see that there were other options out there—and eventually led me to meet a woman who really *was* ready for a connected relationship."

Accept the One You Are

The more self-accepting you are, the more available you will be for genuine intimacy and deep sexual connection with another human being. That's why ideas for growing in self-acceptance—from quieting your self-criticism, to healing from shame or guilt, to learning to express your feelings and desires, to growing more comfortable in your body and with your sexuality—appear in every chapter of this book.

The most important thing to know about self-acceptance is this: *Self-acceptance is a continual process.* You don't need to try to accept yourself completely. You just need to do your best to accept who and where you are right *now*.

As you become more self-accepting, you will find that you naturally treat yourself with more compassion and appreciation. You'll get more in touch with your body and with your ability to see and experience yourself as attractive, desirable, and yes, even sexy. You'll learn to recognize and embrace all of your unique gifts and abilities. You'll be more creative and playful, more open to new ideas and experiences, and more willing to explore and share intimate thoughts, feelings, and desires. All of which will make authentic connection and deeply fulfilling sexual intimacy much easier to create and sustain.

Finding new ways to accept and appreciate yourself is one of the best things you can do for your love life.

207

Accept the One You're With

Practicing acceptance of your partner is just as powerful as practicing acceptance of yourself when it comes to creating an atmosphere for love and intimacy to flourish. It's also a wonderful way to initiate a sexual encounter and to lovingly affirm your connection afterward.

One way to do this is to take a few minutes to just be with each other, with openness and receptivity. Suspend any ideas, assumptions, or beliefs you might be holding about this person. *Be willing to see someone entirely new.* Consciously opening yourself to each other in this way creates a lighter, more loving space between you.

> A state of acceptance is a beautiful place to make love in.
> ༀ

PRACTICE 2:
BE RIGHT HERE, RIGHT NOW

In every moment, you have the choice to be right here, right now, or to be preoccupied by thoughts about the past or the future. When you're feeling upset about something that happened yesterday or worrying about what might happen tomorrow, you won't be able to fully appreciate or make the most of what's happening right now.

This book explores many ways to bring more presence into your relationships, especially your sexual relationships. It offers techniques for shifting your attention away from your mind and back into your body, such as tuning in to your senses and your sexual energy, letting go of sexpectations, and playing at the edge of orgasm. If you ever find yourselves starting to make love on autopilot, go back and review these ideas. Because the more present you and your lover can be with each other, the more intimacy, love, and connection you will naturally experience.

Create Your Own Unknown

When it comes to making love, like almost anything else in life, it's easy to get bored when it's always the same routine. What these moments call for is something new, something "unknown."

You can easily create an experience of the unknown through role-playing. Role-playing isn't necessarily for everyone. But if you happen to be someone whose mind tends to wander off during sex, playing a role will give your mind something worthwhile to do, something that will actually contribute to the intimate experience you're having.

> Being present is the number one secret for ensuring that your sex life continues to be passionate, fulfilling, and fun.

Be the *You* You Want to Be   Have you ever wished you could be different in the bedroom—more confident, more seductive, more creative? Studies have shown that acting as though you have a particular quality can help you to find that quality in yourself. This means you can learn how to *be* the person you want to be by simply playing the role of you *as* that person. Knowing that, don't you think it's time to act?

You might explore a fantasy or desire together, take on roles from a romantic novel or movie that inspires you both, or just be spontaneous. Trying on new roles breaks you free of routine and helps you to approach making love, and each other, with a much more open mind. It encourages you both to bring your full attention, and your entire selves, to the experience you're creating together.

PRACTICE 3:
COME FROM A PLACE OF LOVE

We can classify nearly the entire range of human emotions into two categories: those that are produced when we're in a state of fear and those that are produced when we're in a state of love. In every moment, we have the choice to come from one or the other of these two states.

Doubt, anxiety, guilt, embarrassment, and blame are all forms of fear, as are thoughts of comparison, inferiority, and inadequacy. Fear can manifest as manipulation, jealousy, or resentment. It's fear that compels us to be controlling, judgmental, manipulative, possessive, or deceptive. It's not surprising that we feel most disconnected from other people when we're coming from a state of fear.

Love, on the other hand, manifests as understanding, compassion, honesty, and integrity. It is love that inspires us to be authentic, receptive, kind, and generous. We feel most connected to other people when we're coming from a place of love.

Real intimacy is born from love, not fear. When you're coming

210

from fear, you tend to keep parts of yourself hidden. When you're coming from love, you are more willing to open up and share yourself authentically.

This book explores many ways to recognize when you're operating from a state of fear, and then to shift into a more loving approach. You will find these ideas helpful whether your fear manifests in the form of nervousness about meeting someone new; feelings of doubt, insecurity, or jealousy with a long-term partner; or any kind of sexual anxiety.

> Coming from fear
> separates us.
> Coming from love
> connects us.

One more way to make the shift from fear to love in any situation is to simply ask yourself this question: *How would I be different if I were coming from love right now?* This quick self-inquiry will make it easier to approach almost anything in a more loving, more connected, and more effective way.

Create a Context for Sex

A context is a simple statement of intention that guides you toward greater love, intimacy, and connection. Francine, for example, who has been with her lover, Joy, for several years, has this context for their relationship: "My girlfriend has a great lover." She explains: "Having Joy feel that she has a great lover is really important to me. She's a special woman, and she deserves the best I can give her."

Another context might be "I provide a safe and loving space where we can explore sexually." Or "I make it my job to keep things exciting." Lovers might also create a context together, such as

"Making love is our time to let go of everything else and just enjoy ourselves." A context might even express a higher purpose for your sexual relationship, such as "Our intention for lovemaking is to feel our spiritual connection through our physical connection."

PRACTICE 4:
KNOW THAT WE'RE ALL CONNECTED

In every moment, we have the choice to see ourselves as separate from others or to recognize that we are all connected.

Research in the field of quantum physics has verified that, at the most fundamental level, we're all interconnected: everything that exists is composed of the same energy, and every choice we make will affect ourselves and others in ways we can't possibly predict. The more you recognize the truth that we're all connected, sharing the same basic desires and challenges, the easier it will be to be receptive and authentic—whether with someone you're just getting to know or with your partner of many years.

The exercises that follow can put you and your lover in a very intimate and connected space. And there's no better environment to make love in than that.

Connect Through Your Eyes

When done with awareness, gazing into each other's eyes is more than just a romantic notion. It's a powerful practice for experiencing a deeply intimate sense of connection.

Holding hands if you like, begin looking into each other's eyes. Let go of any effort and just allow yourselves to gaze comfortably. As thoughts arise, instead of following them or holding on to

Eye gazing is like foreplay for the soul.

them, just gently refocus your attention on each other's eyes. Open yourselves to seeing each other, and to being seen, completely.

If you let yourselves relax, you'll notice a shift begin to happen. Issues that might have existed between you, or uncomfortable feelings that were there when you began, may soften or fade away. You might find yourselves experiencing a much deeper sense of each other, an increase in gratitude, and maybe even a rich, satisfying feeling that some people would call pure love or joy.

Connect Through an Embrace

Another way to feel a deep sense of connection is through a hug in which you are both fully present. In a hug like this, which might last for several minutes or more, you each allow yourself to really experience holding the other person and being held by them.

As you begin to hug and start to relax into each other's embrace, allow any feelings of hesitation or resistance to drift away. As thoughts come up, allow them to drift away as well. Take a few breaths into any parts of your body that are carrying tension, consciously relaxing those areas as you exhale. The more you let go, the more you will encourage your partner to also let go.

Notice the rhythm of your partner's breathing. Allow your own breath to synchronize with it. As you continue to let go into one another, you may get the sense that although you came into the embrace as two separate individuals, you are also undeniably connected as one.

PRACTICE 5:
APPRECIATE EVERY MOMENT

In every moment, we have the choice to appreciate life or to be complacent or even to complain about it.

Gratitude is a theme woven throughout the ideas and explorations in this book. We've looked at ways to develop a deeper appreciation of yourself, including your body, your senses, and your sexuality. We've also seen the tremendous gratitude that can result from two people helping each other uncover and heal limiting beliefs or feelings of doubt, shame, or guilt that linger from the past.

It's not surprising that the more gratitude we experience for what we have, the happier, healthier, and more satisfied with our lives and relationships we become. It's easy, however, to fall into the habit of continuously scanning for anything that doesn't measure up to our ideas about how things should be. Making a conscious decision to notice what's right rather than what's wrong is a powerful practice. Whenever you can shift from complaint into gratitude, you instantly experience more harmony and love in your life.

> In the moment you realize that the people you love may not be here tomorrow, you tap into a source of tremendous gratitude.

How do you raise your appreciation for what life is bringing you? By focusing more on being thankful for what you do have than on complaining about what you don't. By recognizing that your time with the ones you love is precious and limited. By noticing when you're about to complain and asking yourself, *What small thing can I be grateful for right now?*

Gratitude on a Soul Level

Is your partner not as interested in exploring your relationship or your sexual connection as you wish they were? Are you navigating some rough waters together? Even at times when you're finding it challenging to feel any gratitude at all toward someone, there's still something you can do: You can appreciate them for being a soul or a spirit in a body, doing the best they can. Or for just being human, with desires, fears, and challenges like everyone else. Or for everything you have learned about relationships and about yourself by being in a relationship with them. Any amount of gratitude will improve your experience, no matter where your relationship goes from here.

If you already have a great relationship, gratitude on a soul level can be both inspiring and healing. By practicing gratitude together, you'll find that you can easily dissolve any feelings of irritation or frustration that may have come up between you, because you'll be able to talk about issues or challenges in a way that stays positive and connected.

Gratitude on a soul level is a sweet, heart-opening practice that can awaken profound feelings of love and compassion between you and your lover. And in an environment filled with love and compassion, anything is possible.

***

As you integrate these five essential practices into your life,
you'll find it much easier to create and sustain a relationship
that is intimate, passionate, and connected on all levels:
body, mind, and soul.

Explorations for Transformation

For your convenience, following is a list of the transformational explorations that appear throughout this book, and the pages on which you will find them.

Questions for Reflection

Use these questions to encourage conversation in a book discussion group after reading each chapter, or simply reflect on them on your own.

Introduction
- What do you hope to get from this book?
- What desires do you have for your intimate relationships?

Chapter 1: Sexy Is a State of Mind
- What are your thoughts or beliefs around the idea of wanting to feel sexy, attractive, or desirable?
- What was your definition of the word *sexy* before you read this chapter?
- What is your definition of *sexy* now?
- What other words, like this one, might you want to redefine for yourself?

Chapter 2: Sensuality Starts with the Senses

- What do you just love the smell of? The taste of? The sound of? The feel of?
- Describe some of the most sensual experiences you've enjoyed with a lover.
- What are some of your "I don't like" beliefs, and where did you acquire them?
- What is one area in which you would be willing to expand your sensory comfort zones?

Chapter 3: Accessing Your Masculine and Feminine Energies

- When you were growing up, what messages did you receive about what it meant to be a boy or a girl? Were you ever told that you couldn't do something, or should do something, solely because of your gender? How has gender conditioning influenced your relationships?
- When have you demonstrated qualities like confidence, will-power, or courage? In what situations might you benefit from being able to access qualities like these? How could you open up more to these types of qualities?
- When have you demonstrated qualities like compassion, receptivity, or intuition? In what situations might you benefit from being able to access qualities like these? How could you open up more to these types of qualities?
- How would you describe the balance of masculine and feminine energies in your current relationship or in past relationships? What might you do to enhance your relationship in this area?

Chapter 4: Letting Go of Sexual Shame

- In what ways, if any, has sexual shame affected your life or your relationships?
- If you have experienced any form of sexual shame, what have you done to work with it? What else might you do?
- What do you imagine a sexual relationship would be like if it were free of feelings of guilt, embarrassment, or shame?

Chapter 5: Inspiration for Getting Off Your A** and Into Your Body

- What inspires you to take care of your body? What gets in the way of taking care of your body?
- What are your favorite ways to let your body play?
- What activity have you tried recently that challenged your body in a new way?
- After reading this chapter, what new ways of motivating yourself are you inspired to try?

Chapter 6: Connecting with Your Sexual Energy

- What did you learn about nudity growing up? How comfortable are you being naked, on your own or with a partner? If you're not comfortable in the nude, what might you do to become more so?
- What did you learn about masturbation as you were growing up? How do you feel about masturbation now?
- How do you connect with your sexual energy, on your own or with a partner?
- Have you experimented with cultivating your sexual energy?
- What is your definition of sexuality? Are there any ways you might expand that definition?

Chapter 7: Seduction, Intimacy, and Keeping the Spark Alive

- What does intimacy mean to you?
- Looking back at your past relationships, how did the intimacy between you and your partners change over time? What would allow you to experience more intimacy or to be more authentic, receptive, and vulnerable in your relationships?
- If you're single, what suggestions for meeting new people are you inspired to try?
- If you're in a relationship, what suggestions for deepening your intimacy are you excited to try?

Chapter 8: Sex and the Practice of Being Present

- How has your ability to be present affected your sexual relationships or experiences?
- What gets in the way of you being present during sex? How could you bring more presence into your sex life?
- What are your feelings about pornography and its effect on people's ability to be present?

Chapter 9: The Power of Invitation

- How have you tried to use manipulation to get what you want in your relationships? How well did it work? How have partners tried to use manipulation to get what they wanted from you, and how well did that work?
- How have you used the power of invitation in your relationships?
- Is there a situation in your life right now where you could use invitation? How could you approach that situation?

Chapter 10: The Art of Sexual Healing

- What are your thoughts about the possibility of lovers using their sexual connection to heal each other?
- What experiences have you had that could be considered sexual healing?
- What situations have you experienced, or are you experiencing, where sexual healing could be helpful? What would that look like?

Chapter 11: Opening Up to Your Orgasmic Potential

- How intimate are you with your anatomy? Is there anything you could do to get more in touch with your own body?
- How would you describe your experiences with orgasm so far?
- How have you practiced cultivating your sexual energy with a partner? After reading this chapter, what suggestions are you inspired to try for opening up to your full orgasmic potential?

Chapter 12: The Five Essential Practices for Truly Soulful Sex

- What could you do to be more self-accepting? How do you practice acceptance with your partner?
- How do you practice being right here, right now? In what ways could you create an experience of the "unknown" with a long-term partner?
- How do you practice coming from a place of love? What context might you create to enhance your sex life?
- When do you feel most connected to your lover? What practices help you, or could help you, to feel more connected?
- How do you tap into your sense of gratitude for your partner? What might you do to increase your appreciation for him or her?

In Gratitude

Reflecting back on the magical four-year adventure of writing this book, we're truly in awe when we consider all the people who so generously shared their experiences, insights, and inspiration. Without their contributions, this book wouldn't be the book it is.

To our children, who have each supported this project in their own unique way: Lana, for your wit, your wisdom, and your infinite patience. You are truly amazing. Sarah, for your eternal optimism and encouragement. And Ben, for your largesse with the fun tickets!

To our coaching clients, for being willing to try new approaches to life's challenges, approaches that often go against popular relationship advice. We are beholden to you for allowing us to share your challenges and your breakthroughs so that others may learn from your experiences.

Anna Embree, our perspicacious and meticulous editor, for so believing in us and our message.

Lisa Vincent, for your sensitivity and wisdom when it comes to matters of the heart.

Abby Minot, our #1 cheerleader, for your infinite wisdom and ability to access it in an instant.

Deanna Dudney, for allowing our readers to benefit from all your "crappy relationship experience."

Michael DeMarchi, for being a radar for love.

Jeanne Hennessy, for opening your home and your heart to us.

Melody Anderson, for keeping it, and us, real.

Dawn Marrero, for always being willing to see the world through new eyes.

Marcie Grambeau, for allowing us to see your light shine.

Marybeth Giefer, for believing in love, magic, and very long engagements.

Suzanne, Patrick, Francesca, and Lucia Callahan, for being our family of guardian angels.

Patricia Bernard and Michael Guen, for sharing your insights into ancient Chinese martial arts.

Ande Lyons, for encouraging us to take on the tough stuff.

Janet Brown, for giving us the perspective we needed.

Claudia Kleiman, for following your intuition.

Rod Bacon, Dominic Colacchio, John Dumitru, Kristi McCullough, Stacey Miceli, Rod Morgan, Sean Mulvihill, Rachel Noyes, Karlyn Pipes, Maile Reilly, Solange Sheppy, Travis Sigley, Guy Tillotson, Porter Weldon, and Lorelei Witte, for the enlightening conversations and your willingness to explore new possibilities.

Bridget Amato, Anna Kyshynska, Wendy Medeiros, Arpita Ohsiek, Arjay Parker, Shannon Sahaja, Lori Salomon, Stephanie Schreiber,

Don Swartz, and Robert Werner, for being teachers of both the physical and the spiritual and always saying just the right words at just the right moment.

Scott Dehn, Robert Frye, Tobin Giblin, Miguel Hernandez, Sid Hutter, Ron Lorensen, Santanu Pani, Mike Pasley, and Sanjay Patel, for being proof that soulful men are alive and well.

Kirstie & Derek Richardson, Michael DiBenedetto & Bernadette Boutros, Gina Hardy & Joel Young, Katharina & Jeromy Johnson, Debbie & Roger Alstad, Amy Zimmer & Jeff Diamond, Ruth & Jim Sharon, and Betsy & Warren Talbot, for your examples of how a conscious intention to stay connected can make a relationship a beautiful and fulfilling place to be.

For inspiration, encouragement, wisdom, and support of all kinds: Laura Alavosus, Jean Arata, Walter Bachtiger, Kerrin Beyers, Matt Beyers, Paul Beyers, Manda Bushnell, Monica Caulfield, Stefani Charren, Roy "The Wine Guru" Chellemi, Cassandra Coffee, René Couret-Lewis, Chas DeFerrari, Laurie Elliott, Leslie Escoto, Marie Franklin, Carmen Gamper, Melissa Gibson, Paul Gilbert, Jessica Goehring, Sophie Golub, Toni Hall, Darin Hemingway, Paul Jabar, Aleah Jordan, Keshni Kamini, Jeff Kelly, Cynthia Martin, Mofrey, Mark Murtaugh, Michael Naumer, Joette Reed, Asia Slowik, Joanne Sprott, Pat Trafton, Karen VanderZee, Max J. Van Praag, Nick Winer, Diane Wismer, and David Woods.

We are grateful for each and every one of you.

Mali & Joe

Index